THE MR X STITCH GUIDE TO CROSS STITCH

First published in 2017

Search Press Limited
Wellwood, North Farm Road,
Tunbridge Wells, Kent TN2 3DR

Text copyright © Jamie Chalmers

Photographs by Stacy Grant

Photographs and design copyright © Search Press Ltd 2017

ISBN: 978-1-78221-424-3

Suppliers
If you have difficulty in obtaining any of the materials and equipment mentioned in this book, then please visit the Search Press website for details of suppliers:
www.searchpress.com

Printed in China by 1010 Printing International Ltd

DEDICATION
To Mary, for keeping it real.
And to the world of cross stitch for allowing me to be its (mostly) humble servant.

SEARCH PRESS

MR X STITCH

LMERS

GUIDE T

CROSS STITC

CONTENTS

Foreword by Julie Jackson	6
Introduction	8

Tools & Materials — 10
Making a start	18
How to cross stitch	20
Framing your work	28
The back	32

Colour — 36
A moment of context	46
Outlier: Zoe Gilbertson	54

Glow in the Dark — 56
Stitching and travelling	63
Outlier: Kate Blandford	72

More Than a Hobby — 74
Peace of mind	76
Embroidery as therapy	79
Craftivism	83
Embroidery as an art form	86
Outlier: Severija Inčirauskaitė-Kriaunevičienė	90

Pattern Design — 92
Computer design	94
Fabric count	99
Colour	100

Epic pineapple	102
Outlier: Lord Libidan	116

Thinking Outside the Hoop — 118
If it's got holes in it...	120
Stitching on plastic	122
Stitching on metal	127
We're all adults	131
Outlier: Les Deuz'Bro	132

Final thoughts — 134
Alphabet fonts	136
Acknowledgements	140
Index	141

PROJECTS

Back in Black	32
Fleur de Couleur	40
From Ampersand to Bargello	42
Something Meaningful	47
Sqrl!	50
Empire State	58
Winter is Coming	64
Home Sweet Home Network	68
VodkAtomic	70
I Got Yer Mindfulness Right Here	76
I am an Addict	80
#StitchforSyria	83
Mona	87
Introducing the Pineapple!	95
Portrait of a Pineapple	104
Pop Art Pineapple	108
Whitby Abbey at Sunset	112
Bling	120
Silver Devil	124
C-Tron	125
Yellow Blade	126
Look!	127
What The?!	128

FOREWORD

Back in 2003 when I started Subversive Cross Stitch, I had no idea where cross stitch was headed and little time to think about it very much. Most of the stitching world was still stuck with old-fashioned, sappy-sweet samplers and the cool kids were just starting to get into knitting. Online communities for crafting were scant, with all kinds of crafts piled together in a tangled mess. Articles about the craft movement were virtually unheard of.

I can't remember exactly how I first learned about Jamie and his plans for mrxstitch.com, but I do remember my unbridled enthusiasm. We talked and talked and even Skyped and toured each other's homes and lives (something I've never shared with any other colleague, ever). Here was this big British guy stitching on trains just because he loved cross stitch. He gave me so much hope for the future!

In the years that followed, Jamie has created a central online repository for all things cross stitch. I have watched in pure amazement as he has built his site and enlisted so many talented contributors to cover the modern cross stitch movement. For years, I've sent countless people to his site because it truly is the only place that covers just about everything stitch-related. I used to send him links to stories online I thought he should cover, but now I find he's already covered those stories. Jamie is so on top of his game and his ability to curate is very impressive.

His sense of humour and ability to step into the spotlight and speak with authority continues to wow me. Watching his TED Talk[1] is a thrill – especially because I could never stand up in front of people and speak, much less make the crowd laugh, and think. Jamie – and by extension, his site – is inviting, enthusiastic and shatters the outdated idea that stitching is only for women of a certain age.

It's been exciting to watch Jamie build his online empire. And, of course, someone with the ability to absorb so much is the best person to write a book on the subject. This book is thorough, thoughtful and packed with encouragement and enthusiasm to take us into the future of cross stitch.

Julie Jackson
Subversive Cross Stitch

1 TED is a nonprofit devoted to spreading ideas, usually in the form of short, powerful talks (18 minutes or less). TED began in 1984 as a conference where Technology, Entertainment and Design converged, and today covers almost all topics, from science to business to global issues, in more than 100 languages.

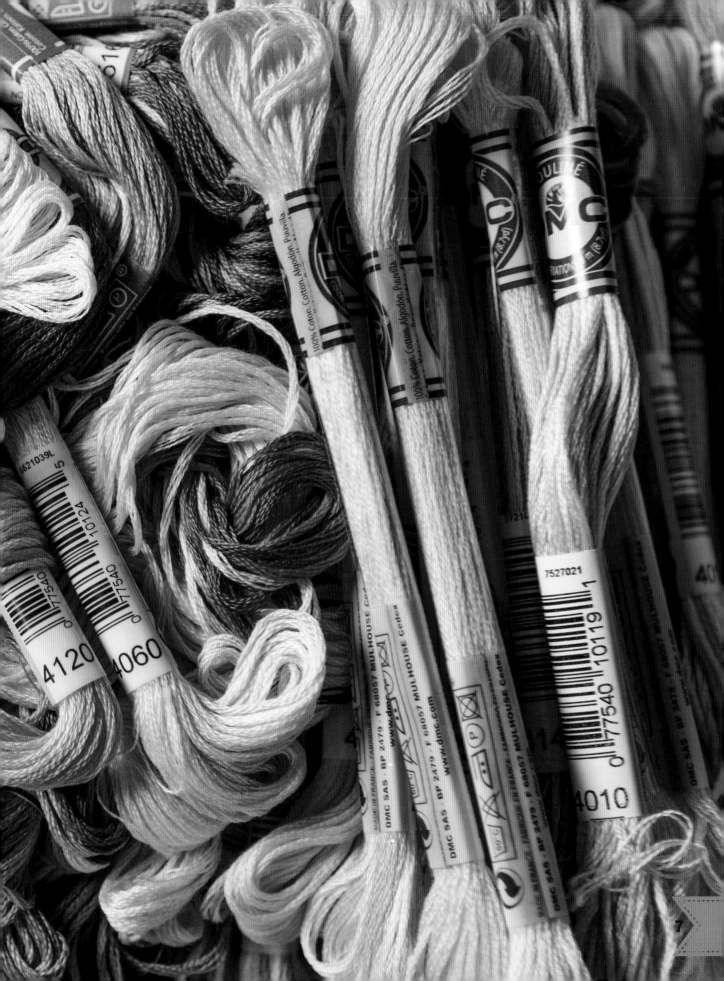

INTRODUCTION

Welcome to *The Mr X Stitch Guide to Cross Stitch*. Inside these pages you'll find all the tools, techniques and tips you need to become a thriving cross stitcher. Cross stitch is an embroidery technique that is known and enjoyed throughout the world. It's a simple stitch that has the power to change lives. It has benefits that go far beyond the pleasure of creating hand-made art.

I'm Jamie Chalmers, aka Mr X Stitch, aka the Kingpin of Contemporary Embroidery, and it's my absolute pleasure to introduce you to the wonderful world of cross stitch. I've been cross stitching for 15 years, and it's fair to say that it has changed my life in numerous ways. After discovering the soul-soothing secret of those little Xs, I began creating my own patterns and in 2008 launched Mr X Stitch, the world's best contemporary embroidery and needlecraft site. I didn't realise what I'd stumbled into.

At Mr X Stitch, we don't do knitting and we don't do dressmaking, but we cover all other forms of needlecraft, from quilting to millinery, from needle felting to machine embroidery, from plush toys to lace and much more. I'm honoured to work with a stellar list of co-authors, each of whom curate content from around the world to share their love of textile art with you. We take this stuff seriously, but not too seriously, so we occasionally have NSFW (Not Safe For Work) Saturdays, featuring the saucier side of stitching, and we often have Stitchgasms, where embroidery produces a visceral response, usually followed by a short nap!

We've got thousands of posts on all kinds of needlework, and it's amazing to see how vibrant the world of needlework, and indeed cross stitch, has become. Across the globe people are exploring cross stitch in new and fun ways, whether it's pop culture references or stunning visuals, so if you're interested in any type of needlecraft, you ought to be following us on the internet, because you will be inspired!

The aim of *The Mr X Stitch Guide to Cross Stitch* is to teach you how to cross stitch, share some of the key features of the world of cross stitch and encourage you to become a cross stitch designer. It's remarkable how much potential for creativity can be found within this simple stitch, and I'll introduce some of my favourite cross stitch Outliers – people who are pushing at the frontiers of this art form – so you can learn what is possible with cross stitch and use that knowledge to make your world a better place.

I hope you enjoy the book, I hope you enjoy the process of stitching and that it unlocks your creativity, while giving you a nice handmade present for someone special as well.

One more thing before you read this book, and particularly if you've never cross stitched before – take a moment to stop and look at the world around you. Take it all in and know that your life is about to change forever.

Are you ready? Let's go!

Jamie aka Mr X Stitch

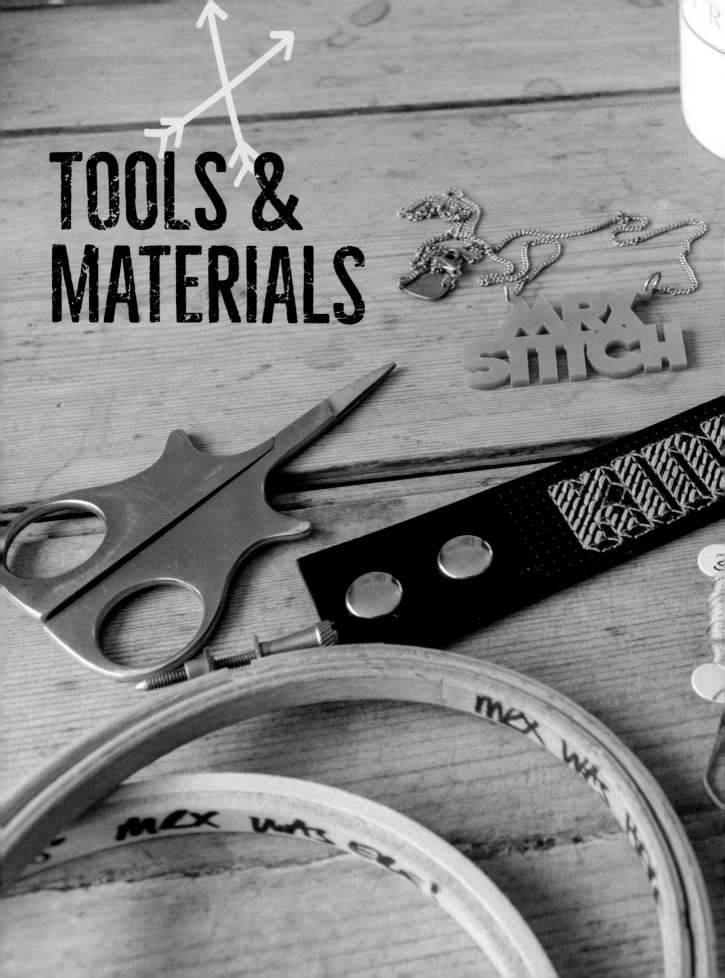

TOOLS & MATERIALS

TOOLS & MATERIALS

To know your craft, you must first know your tools...

NEEDLES

The needle is to the stitcher as the katana is to the Samurai warrior and, as needlecraft ninjas, it is important that you know your weapons and choose the right ones for your battles. You might think I'm being a bit dramatic, but if any of you have completed a Heaven and Earth design, you know what an epic achievement it is.

Made from steel, needles come in a range of sizes and types, depending on the work you're doing. Generally speaking, cross stitch is done using tapestry needles, which have a slightly rounded point with a large eye. The sizes range from 13 and 14, which are ideal for younger stitchers working with Binca and other low-count fabrics (see page 14), up to 22 to 28, that are most commonly used for cross stitch. Generally speaking, with needles, the higher the number, the finer the needle.

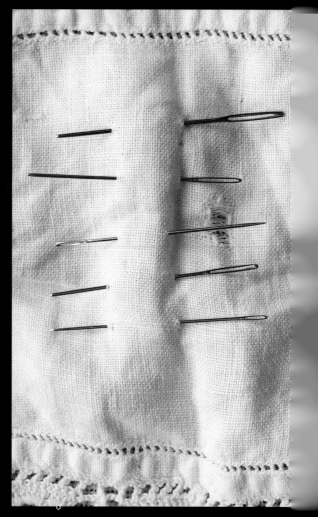

If you're looking to embellish your work, or branch out into ribbon work, crewel or other hand embroideries, you may choose to use embroidery needles; however, the sharper ends (ideal for piercing fabrics) are more likely to catch on the irregular surface of Aida or evenweave and can often slow you down.

If you've a big design and time pressures, you could try the John James Twin Pointed Quick Stitch needle, which has the eye in the middle with two ends. It's great for people using a frame, as you can use a shuttle motion to push the needle up and down without turning it, shaving micro-seconds off each stitch. I've used twin-pointed needles in the past and you can get a good pace going if you're using them (and listening to some cracking drum and bass music at the same time).

If you're feeling fancy, you can use gold-plated needles, whose surface holds the thread and works with the fabric in a subtly different way. It's really hard to explain, but they're slightly better. And they are a bit more gangsta, so I like 'em!

Just remember, needles are sharp and metallic, and they're not good for swallowing or sticking in flesh, so be sure that you know where you put them when you're done! There's nothing wrong with a pincushion in your life.

THREADS

Embroidery thread, or floss, is the main ingredient in your stitching system. There's a huge amount of variety in colour and texture, from bamboo floss to silk thread, as well as metallic and glow-in-the-dark versions.

Most threads are made from cotton, and dyed using industrial dipping processes. The two main thread manufacturers, DMC and Anchor, have hundreds of colours for you to choose from, as well as offering variegated varieties if you're feeling funky. I've used DMC threads for all my designs.

As with most good things in life, you can find fancy artisanal threads if you look hard enough, and it can be really pleasing to buy hand-dyed silks from a local producer. Companies such as Kreinik offer shiny, sparkly and metallic threads for you to add glitz to your work.

Generally speaking, embroidery floss comes in skeins that are over eight yards long, with six strands per skein. In most cases you'll use two strands of thread for stitching and one for backstitching, although if you're using dark fabrics, a three-ply option will make your stitching thicker and hide the background.

Separating the strands

There are a few ways of separating your strands of thread, but here's my trusted method for doing it without too much kerfuffle.

1 Take the floss between your thumb and forefinger and spread the strands apart.

2 Find the one you want and pull it, while holding the other strands between your thumb and forefinger. As long as the strand isn't too long, it should come out without a hitch.

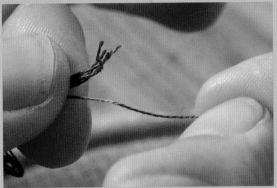

Try to resist the temptation to pull out more than one strand at once, as it'll probably get tangled up. Most of the time you won't want to cut your thread to longer than the length of your forearm, as that's the maximum stitching motion your arm will give you, unless you're a stretchy superhero. The exception to this rule is if you're using the Loop Technique to start (see page 22), but even then, you don't want too long a thread as it'll be more hassle than it's worth.

FABRIC

To ensure a consistent cross stitch structure, it's important to have a grid pattern of holes that you can use to stitch through. There are quite a few ways to achieve this and we'll look at some of the more unorthodox surfaces later in the book. Let's start with the simple stuff.

While there are numerous surfaces you could stitch on, generally we go for fabric as the medium of choice and with cross stitch there are some very specific fabrics ideal for our purposes.

Cross stitch fabric can be broadly classified as evenweave, as there are a consistent number of threads per inch in both width and length (or warp and weft, to use the correct terms), also known as thread count. However, not all evenweaves are Even Weave, and you can also use Aida, linen, Binca or needlepoint canvas. More often than not, evenweave and linen fabrics use a 1:1 thread ratio, so the holes you stitch would feature at the intersection of each thread. If you want to stitch on linen, you'd probably need to use a single strand of thread and some magnification, as that 1:1 ratio could potentially equate to 32 stitches per inch!

Aida is the most common cross stitch fabric. It was developed in 1907 by Zweigart with the four warp and weft threads being woven to produce an openwork effect. Aida is available in a range of thread counts (stitches per inch) from 6 to 20, and there is a myriad of colours available.

Thanks to innovations in digital printing, it's now possible to get your Aida pre-printed with all manner of designs, and I'd like to give a shout out to my chums at sewitall.com who have a groovy glow-in-the-dark Aida in their arsenal. Many of the designs in this book are stitched on black, but none of the fabric choices are too prescriptive – stitch them on whatever colour you like!

A good tip when using black fabric is to have something light behind it – a piece of paper will do – so that you can see the holes that bit better. It'll help keep eye strain to a minimum.

Waste canvas is a useful material as it can be placed onto any fabric, and once you've stitched your design onto it you can pull out the threads of the canvas, leaving the stitching directly on the fabric. It is invaluable as it allows you to stitch cross stitch onto non-evenweave fabrics by providing the grid you need for consistent stitches.

As well as waste canvas, you can also get **paper interface** that provides the grid for stitching and can be removed after you've finished. **Soluble plastic interface** is the other alternative, which dissolves in warm water when you're finished, but can leave a residue on the stitches, making them a bit stiff. If you're going to use the plastic, be sure to rinse it out well.

GIZMOS

I love a good gizmo and, although I have managed to restrain myself from buying all the new tools that come out, I thought I'd share a few that I think you'll like.

Bobbin box

If you've got more than a dozen threads on the go, it's worth investing in a bobbin box and some bobbins to keep everything in check. While it's a bit time-consuming winding your skeins up, the use of a bobbin winder will speed up the process, and it is extremely satisfying to end up with a box of well-organised threads. The only challenge then is how you organise them – by colour or by number?

Scissors

You're gonna need some blades if you want to cut your threads and there are lots of different types of scissors that you can choose from. However, when indulging in needlework it's useful to have a fine-pointed blade for getting underneath stitches that need removing, and it's quite nice to have a magnetic tip that'll pick up needles and pins. If you can, try to keep your scissors just for needlework and let other pairs around the house deal with the other cutting chores. One of my favourite pairs are the Total Control Scissors (see photograph on page 16), which give you more contact points for holding them, allowing for more precision; however, I also like them because they look like an electric guitar, adding to that rock star image I'm desperately clinging to.

Laying tool

For a nice finish to your work you'll want your stitches to lie nice and flat, and the best way to get this effect is by using a laying tool (see above, right). 'Railroading' is a technique whereby your stitches lie parallel to each other, much like train tracks, and a laying tool helps achieve this by stabilising the stitches as you pull them. You can use a needle to the same end, but if you're taking this stuff seriously, a metal or wooden laying tool is a must. (They're also quite handy for scratching your ears!)

15

Thread cutter

When you're travelling you might want to take a thread cutter, rather than some scissors, to avoid any confusion about safety. While there are quite a few types of cutter, I really like the ring made by ThreadCutterz, which sits on your finger and contains two blades that'll cut through most threads with ease.

Thread conditioner

If you're using shiny threads or metallic threads, you might find that they don't always behave themselves, either coming loose or getting stuck on the fabric.

Thread Heaven is a conditioner that protects your threads with a fine layer of PH neutral coating, making shiny threads a bit more adhesive and making metallic threads a bit smoother. It's a really useful thing to have if you're getting glitzy with your stitching.

Needle minder

Take a couple of strong magnets, put a nice surface on the top of one of them and you've got a needle minder! These are handy as the magnets mean you can stick them to your fabric and keep your needles in one place while stitching. They're a handy alternative to a...

Pincushion

If you've got children or pets, you might not want to take them to the doctors or vets to have needles removed. So get a pincushion. You can buy them in all kinds of colours and sizes and a tiny bit of money spent on a cushion may save you a buck or two in the future.

Light

When you're young and invulnerable you'll probably be able to cross stitch in the middle of a nightclub, with the bassline rhythms helping your needle make its way across the fabric, but as you get older, it becomes important to think about light.

You will save yourself a lot of time and potential headaches if you stitch in well-lit conditions. Daylight is the best, with a good indoor spotlight coming a close second for those people who keep their stitching at home. I've experimented with a few ideas over time and here's a whistle-stop summary of what I've learned:

If you're stitching with a frame there are various clip-on lights that you can try. Key things to look out for are flexibility (the ability to position the light in the direction you need it), portability (how cumbersome it is on and off the frame) and power. With the latter, battery-operated models offer mobility, whereas a plug-in light keeps you near a plug socket, but at least the batteries won't run out.

If you don't use a frame, it's good to get near a lamp at the very least. If you can get away with it, using a daylight light bulb will help you see the colour differences. If you use a clip-on battery lamp, then think about getting rechargeable batteries to go with it. You don't notice when the batteries start to fade but you'll be stitching in the dark again if you're not careful.

If you have the budget, it's worth investing in a dedicated stitching lamp and, again, daylight lights will be your best purchase. I use the Daylight Company's Slimline LED lamp, which has a long flexible arm while also having a discreet design that doesn't look odd in my living room.

For the maverick among you, a head torch is a handy way of getting light when you need it. Just remember to take it off before you go out for the day!

MAKING A START

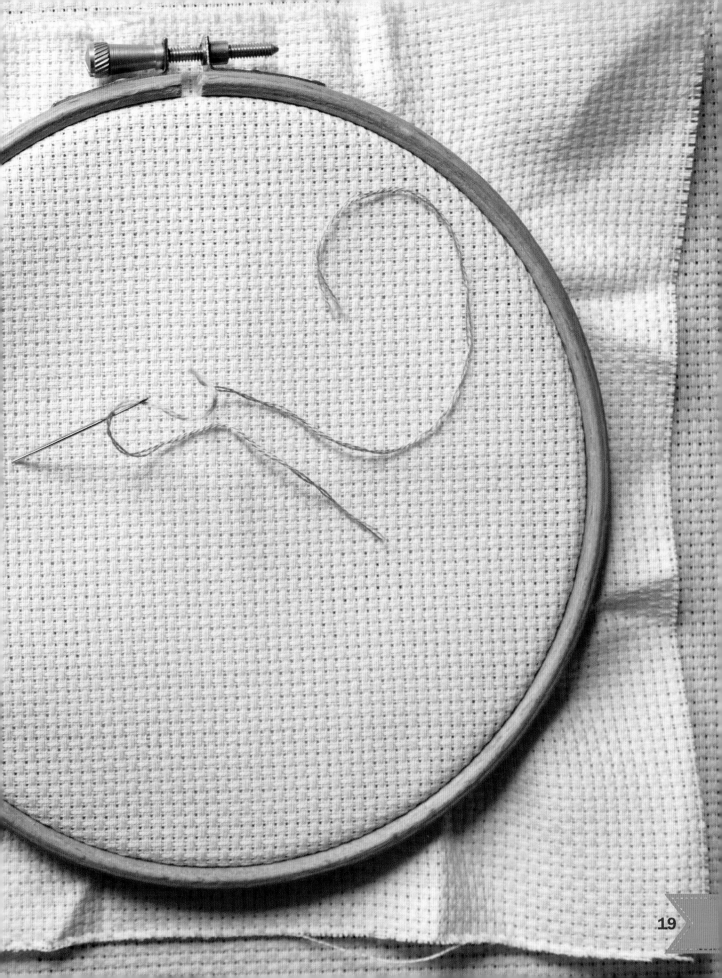

HOW TO CROSS STITCH

Brace yourselves, people, this is where it gets real!

Cross stitch is made of two stitches, a bottom stitch and a top stitch, and I always talk about forward slashes and backslashes: //// and \\\\.

There's only one rule about cross stitch – try to make sure your bottom stitch goes in the same direction. So you might do forward slashes for the bottom and backslashes for the top, or vice versa. As long as you stick with this principle, your cross stitch will look nice and even in terms of texture.

(Psst! Even this rule can be broken, and there's nothing wrong with it. If you're a brain surgeon or airline pilot, please adhere to the rules you're given, but if you're a cross stitcher, well – no one is gonna die if you stitch it however you want.)

When it comes to following cross stitch patterns, essentially it's like painting by numbers, as you will have a design with a colour code attached, and you count the number of stitches of each colour as you stitch. If it's a design that will take a long time, it's often wisest to stitch the colours from dark to light, so that any dirt you pick up along the way is less likely to show up.

When starting a design, you want to pick a section of colour that's close to the centre and stitch it, moving to similarly coloured sections as you go. I'll talk about this principle in more detail later on, but find yourself the bit you want to stitch and get ready. So let's crack on!

You will need:

✗ Fabric
✗ Threads
✗ Needle
✗ Embroidery hoop (optional, but recommended)
✗ Some water (optional, but it's good to be hydrated)
✗ Whatever else you need to be comfortable.

Now that you're set, let's get a-stitching!

First off, we'll get the fabric in your hoop.

1 It's good practice to fold the fabric in half both ways, and put a little crease in the centre, as this will help you identify the middle of the pattern. So fold one way...

2 ... and then the other way. Most large patterns will show you where the centre is, and believe me, it's super annoying to run out of room on your fabric, so it's important to start in the middle and work outwards. All being well, if you've got the right size, the design will fit on the fabric as you like it.

3 So, now that you can see the centre point on your fabric, place it centrally over the inner ring of the embroidery hoop, then press the outer ring down around the inner ring, making sure there is an overlap all the way round. It should fit snugly. As you tighten the screw to hold it securely in place, adjust the fabric so that it is taut and smooth. There should be no puckering or looseness.

The Loop Technique

With the fabric in place, next up it's the thread.

On the Thread page I explained that you won't really need a piece longer than your forearm, and I showed how to separate your floss strands, so refer to page 13 and then come back to me.

You back? Right, then.

refer to page 13

tip When I'm stitching, I tend to have the tip of the needle near the tip of my forefinger, as it's easier to find the hole I need when rooting around on the reverse. I usually press the eye of the needle against my middle finger, as it holds the thread in place and reduces the chance of it slipping out.

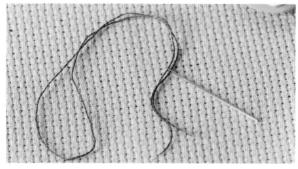

1 The first technique we'll use to get stitching is the Loop Technique. For this you'll want to take a single strand of thread, fold it in half and put both ends through the needle by at least 5cm (2in). You should end up with something like this (see left).

2 You should know where you want to start stitching, so start by poking the needle from underneath through your desired hole, and then do your first forward slash by moving diagonally up and to the right to the next available hole. Pull the thread through, but not all the way, and with the first stitch only, turn the hoop over and put the needle through the loop on the back. This will anchor the thread in place in a super tidy way. Clever, huh?

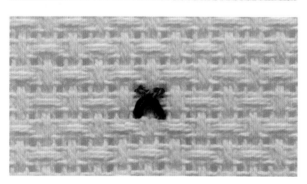

3 To complete the stitch, simply do a backslash from the top left hole of your 'square' to the bottom right, and hey presto, you've got an X.

You'll always have two holes that you can enter when making a stitch, going from top to bottom or bottom to top, and on the whole it doesn't matter which way you go. There may be a natural direction that you're stitching in, depending on your design, so your stitches might follow that.

You might find that you've already used one hole with a previous stitch, in which case you'll have to use the other one. The best thing to do is not overthink it and you'll work it out. Don't worry if your bottom stitch is a forward slash, or a backslash, just do whichever one comes naturally, and then continue with that as your bottom stitch throughout.

The Waste Knot Technique

If I'm following a pattern, I will often complete a particular section using bottom stitches only, as it's the bit that involves counting and concentration. Once I've completed the section, I can go back on myself with the top stitches, without having to count, and therefore having a less stressful existence.

The other common method of starting is called the Waste Knot Technique. This is useful if you don't have a long thread and therefore a loop to use – if you're using the same bit of thread in a different section, for instance.

With the Waste Knot Technique, you'll want two strands of threads, no longer than your forearm, and you'll tie a knot in the end. This can be done by wrapping the thread around the end of your finger, rolling the thread off and then pulling the end. All being well, the thread should form a knot big enough to stop the end of the thread from getting through the holes in the fabric.

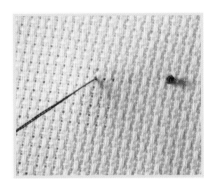

1 You have to work out what direction you'll be stitching in – right to left, up to down, whatever – and then you'll place your knot away from the section you're stitching, but in the direction that you'll be stitching. Bear with me on this...

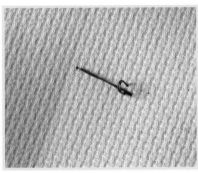

2 You plunge your needle through the fabric from the top side, and the knot will hold the thread in place. You'll then move to the place where your first stitch will be and come up from beneath to do your bottom stitch.

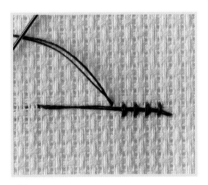

3 You'll notice that the thread has been held along the underside of the fabric, and as you start stitching, in the direction of the knot, your stitches will start securing that thread in place (the technical term is couching).

4 Once you've made a few stitches, you should be able to pull your knot gently upwards and snip it off, with the thread held in place by your new stitches.

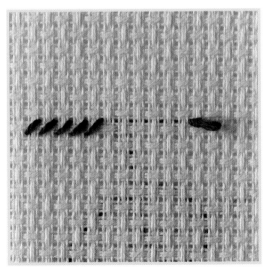

5 It sounds complicated, but it isn't. Just remember that you want to stitch in the direction of the knot, so your initial knot placement is important.

Finishing off

The Circle of Life means that all things must come to an end, and the same is true for cross stitch. At some point, you'll either run out of thread, or come to the end of the section you're stitching, and therefore you'll want to secure your stitches.

To do so, all you need to remember is to 'Wheedle The Needle', as shown in the steps below. (A point of note: I'm in the process of trademarking the phrase 'Wheedle The Needle' so if you use the words Wheedle, The or Needle, you might owe me 50p.)

tip So you've got to grips with the basic X of the cross stitch and, between you and me, there ain't a heck of a lot more to learn. It is ridiculously simple. The main things to remember are to make sure you put the needle through the holes, rather than piercing the fabric, and that you don't pull your stitches too tight, as it can cause unnecessary tension.

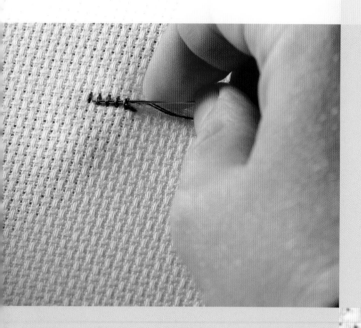

1 Take your needle and wheedle it under three or four stitches on the underside of your work.

2 Pull the thread through and snip off the excess. You should find that the thread will be held by the stitches and is nicely tucked away. Simple, huh?!

BACKSTITCH

Backstitch is used throughout embroidery and is the simple application of a straight stitch to a piece of work. It can be highly effective in cross stitch as it allows detail to be added to the pixelated image, crisping up designs and adding character. There's nothing nicer than finishing all the cross stitches and then busting out the backstitch to tidy up a piece and, as you will see later on in the book, I like to use it to add a 3D effect to words and images. Backstitching is your friend and you should learn to love it.

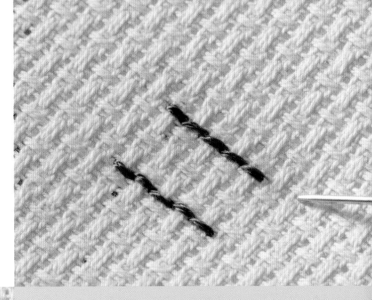

Backstitching is fairly straightforward (or backward, if we're nitpicking) and there's only one point of note when making straight lines in backstitch. Try to ensure that your thread runs from the top of one stitch to the bottom of the next (as illustrated in the top row above). That is, each hole will have two threads entering it, and if they are stitched without due diligence, sometimes the stitch will sit above and below its neighbours (as in the bottom row above), which creates a less smooth finish when seen from a distance.

You might need to trust me on this one, but if you're able to take the time to place your backstitches as shown in the top row of the image, it'll look nicer.

25

SNIPPETS OF WISDOM

So there you have it. I've explained how to start, how to stop, and what to do in the middle.
As long as you take your time and count carefully you should be okay.
But here are a few snippets of wisdom to guide you on your way.

Because you're using a continuous thread when you're stitching, it makes sense to think about the journey you'll take when stitching different sections of the same colour. You don't want to make big jumps between spaces if you can help it, as it's really easy to miscount and stitch things in the wrong place. If you've two sections of the same colour near one another, work out the shortest jump between the two and direct the path of your stitching so that you end up at that point.

Sometimes you can stitch a section with bottom stitches, and then double back, but at other times, the design might necessitate doing both bottom and top stitches as you go. This will become clear as you get stitching, as there will naturally be some elements that you won't want to double back on. Conversely, you might find that there are some elements that you have to stitch and then double back on, to avoid stitching yourself into a corner, as it were.

If you've got a big piece to stitch, you might consider using a single strand of a bright colour to mark every 10 rows and columns with a simple running stitch. It might take a bit of time at the start but it could save hours of unpicking!

You might also want to protect the edges of your fabric from fraying. You can do this by using either a running stitch to add some strength or, if the fabric edges won't be on show, some decorator's tape folded over the edges will do the job. Take care when using tape, as you want something low-tack that won't prove problematic when you come to remove it.

Sometimes a pattern will have a lot of different colours for you to play with, and there are some hefty designs in the latter pages of this book. Often times you'll be stitching a few squares of one colour, a few of another and you won't necessarily want to be finishing those threads off, so you need to learn about parking.

Parking your threads is a way of positioning the remaining thread approximately where you'll need it in the future, so that it doesn't get caught up in the current bit of stitching you're doing. It's one of those things that's really complicated to explain, but not difficult to do. When you're stitching a section, and you've got threads to park, you don't want them to be too close to the section you're working on; once you've stitched the particular colour, look to see where you'll be using it next and then place a bottom stitch of the thread roughly in that area. That will keep the thread that's on the back out of the way and minimise the risk of it getting caught up.

If you're working on highly detailed designs, you'll want to get to grips with parking as it's most helpful, so search for the subject on YouTube and see how other people do it to find your own way.

With big pieces that you know will take time, it's often a good idea to start with the dark colours and work towards the lighter ones. You're bound to get some dirt on the piece at some point, even if it's just dust or grease, and the dark colours can hide these misdemeanours better than the light ones.

If you're working on a large design that is predominantly one colour range – blues and greens, for example – there's no harm in having a design with an alternative colour palette, maybe reds and yellows, so that you can switch between them to avoid colour-based boredom.

Washing your work

Once your stitchery is finished, you'll probably want to wash it for a variety of reasons:

✗ Dirt and grime are inevitable, unless you're in a vacuum or you finished the thing in an hour. Whether it's the grease from your hands or that spilled cup of tea (what were you thinking?!), you're bound to have a few stains in there.

✗ Hair and other bits of fluff can get enmeshed in your designs and, while this kind of washing isn't very vigorous, it should help shift some of them.

✗ Hoop marks can arise from the pressure of fabric against wooden hoop for a sustained period.

Giving your work a brief wash is a good way to make sure that the threads are as fresh-looking as you intended, and will also give you a better chance at getting any creases out as well. Here's what the team at DMC threads have to say on the subject of washing. This book only uses DMC threads, so their advice seems pretty relevant! Here it is:

✗ Always wash each cross-stitched piece separately. Do not wash with any other embroidery project or laundry items.

✗ Wash in cold water (tap water is fine unless you have very hard water, then you will want to use distilled water). Make sure the sink and any containers you will use are clean.

✗ Pre-rinse the piece under cold running water.

✗ Mix in a small amount of mild detergent or dishwashing liquid and wash gently. Do not use specially formulated wool wash, harsh detergents, or chlorine bleach.

✗ Rinse several times in cold water. Do not worry if water becomes coloured when washing, continue rinsing piece until water runs clear.

✗ Roll the piece between two clean towels, squeezing gently without wringing. Do not allow the embroidery to touch upon itself.

✗ Unroll towels and spread flat to dry on a fresh towel or drying rack. Let the piece air dry until it is just damp but not dripping wet so that it can be ironed.

✗ To iron your washed piece, place the cross stitch face down between two clean towels (the towels protect your stitches from being crushed) and press lightly with a warm iron. *Never* use a hot iron.

✗ To remove creases or fold lines use the steam setting on your iron.

✗ Do not use protective coating sprays or other products of this type on your cross-stitched piece as they may cause a chemical reaction with the thread dyes.

✗ It is not recommended that your cross-stitched piece be dry cleaned.

So that's the best practice. Ignore it at your peril! Well, ignore it carefully, but take the time to dampen and press your work if you can – it's worth the effort!

FRAMING YOUR WORK

You've stitched the thing, you've washed the thing and you've pressed the thing. Now it's time to frame the thing!

Finding the right frame to complement your stitching is a skill and the only advice I can really give is to spend time searching off- and online to find the ones you want, and then keep that info in a safe place for future reference. When you find a source of sweet frames it can be a right result as there's a lot of choice out there, and that isn't always a good thing.

There are many ways to get your work in a position to be hung on a wall, whether it's framing it in a hoop, making a wood frame from scratch or buying an existing frame from a shop. Let's have a quick spin through these ideas.

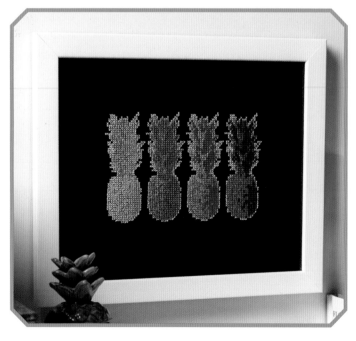

Wooden embroidery hoop

I've used wooden hoops, also known as hooplas, as frames for a lot of my work in the past as I like the simple elegance of a circle of wood. It can be a quick win; you can make sure the fabric is securely in the frame, and that the embroidery is centred and then trim it to suit.

If the back of your work looks messy and you're getting kinda stressy, place another piece of fabric behind it before securing the frame and you'll be able to hide all manner of sins.

If you want something a bit more elegant, you can trim your fabric so that it overhangs the hoop by about 2.5cm (1in), and then use a simple running stitch to pleat the fabric around the hoop to create a nice finish.

Don't be afraid to paint the hoop to suit its surroundings, but make sure it's dry before you use the fabric, and consider varnishing it to be confident that the paint won't rub off.

And finally, it's worth using a screwdriver to make sure that the hoop is nice and tight. If the fabric starts slipping over time, that ain't good!

Making your own frame

There's a lot of skill in making picture frames and I don't have the space to impart those skills in this book (not least because I don't have those skills!), but if you have the ability to make your own frames, it can unlock all manner of possibilities.

It can be quite limiting to use existing frames, and quite expensive to get frames made professionally for big pieces, and although it takes some skill and some specialist equipment, it's not all that difficult to level up to be able to make your own frames. If you're serious about your stitching, you might consider learning to make frames, as it'll save you a fortune in the long term.

Using existing frames

The easiest way to get work into frames is to use existing ones, and whether it's cheap and cheerful frames from a craft shop, or antique frames from a thrift store, the right frame will elevate your work and make it a lovely piece of home décor.

If you're making work from scratch, there's a bit of wisdom in knowing what frame sizes are available, so that you won't run out of space with either your fabric or your frame.

Don't be afraid to upcycle frames with a coat of paint or some nifty decoupage to give them a new lease of life, and be sure to varnish them to seal the deal (pun intended).

Whether it's an old frame or a new bespoke frame, it's important that you treat your embroidery with the right TLC so that it looks good in the frame. You don't want a wonky weave or a slipped stitchery, so we'll use the lattice method of stretching the fabric to fit good and proper (see page 30).

Before we start, one important point. Never glue your work into a frame or onto a surface! You'll regret it at some point and it'll ruin the work in the long term. Just trust me on that – you don't need to find out for yourself!

The Lattice Method

This technique uses thread to stretch fabric over a piece of card in a lattice pattern, not dissimilar to lacing a bodice, so that the fabric is evenly stretched without warping.

When you have your frame, the first step is to get a robust piece of cardboard – cereal boxes are strong enough but not too thick. Using the glass from the frame, cut the cardboard to size. If you don't have glass, use the aperture of the frame as the template for your card. You want the card to be a close fit, but with a bit of room for the fabric.

The back of the design

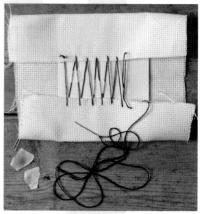

1   With your washed and pressed piece of fabric, position the card on the centre of the rear and trim your fabric so that there's between 2.5–5cm (1–2in) excess. The size of the excess should proportionally relate to the size of the frame – this will make sense later. Position the card in the centre and fold the fabric over the longest edges, creasing them to make sure they fit correctly.

2   Now for the threading! Use all six strands of floss with this method, as you want some strength, and start by cutting at least 60cm (2ft) of thread. Knot it and thread it through the needle. Starting about 1cm (⅜in) in from the short edge of the card, begin sewing the long sides together, from one to the other. Keep the stitches fairly close together – around 1cm (⅜in) apart – to maintain a good tension.

3   After half a dozen stitches, check that the tension is even and that the fabric is stretched tightly over the card. Use a bit of masking tape to stick the threads to the back of the card and then cut and knot the thread, making sure the knot is tight to the fabric. Continue this process until you've latticed the two sides together. Check that the stitched design is centred on the fabric; if it needs adjusting, peel the masking tape from the card and tweak as needed. Hopefully your knots will keep the threads from unravelling.

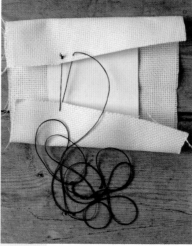

Now it's time to stitch the shorter sides, using the same technique, but before you do that, it's important to tidy your corners! If you have too much excess fabric on the remaining edges, trim it down a bit as you want to minimise the thickness of your folded corners. Then fold your corners and if required, tape them down.

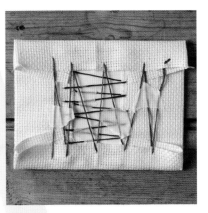

4 Then, believe it or not, follow the same lattice stitching to stitch the other two sides in place, adjusting the finished piece once you're done.

5 If everything has gone according to plan, you should end up with a nicely centred, flat design that's evenly stretched over your card. From there you can assemble it into the frame, adding the glass if necessary and sealing the back.

Hurrah! You've done it! A cross stitch that's finished, washed, pressed and framed and ready to give to a friend or loved one to make them cry. What could be better than that?!

Of course, not all cross stitch needs to be framed and stuck on a wall, and later in the book we'll look at ways of thinking outside the hoop. But before we move on to a new section, there's one more topic that we need to talk about and it can be one of the most stressful ideas in the whole world of cross stitch. Are you sitting comfortably? Then turn over the page...

THE BACK...

If ever there was a subject that strikes fear into the heart of any fledgling stitcher, it's the back of your work.

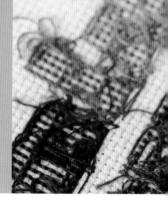

There's a myth going around town, an urban legend that says the back of your work should be as neat as the front. Usually started by a friend of a friend who knew an old lady with loads of cross stitch, who said that unless your back is really tidy, you'll be sent to hell and your children will all have gills. I might be paraphrasing, but I thought I'd dispel this myth for you here and now. Take a deep breath.

It's nice to keep your work neat. It makes life easier when stitching and it means that work will lie a bit flatter on any surface you choose. Backs with lots of knots and tangles can be unruly, but – and this is the important bit – we are talking about cross stitch, not heart surgery. So it doesn't really matter how bad the back is, because it's the back. Most of the time you can hide it somehow, if it's making you feel uncomfortable.

The back of your work shows the journey you've taken to make the front. It's fun to look at the backs and see when tangles have happened and how many jumps between patches of colour people have made with the same thread. You can gain a sense of whether the piece was plain sailing, or whether there was any wailing or gnashing of teeth.

There are some forms of embroidery, such as Shadow Embroidery, where the back of the work is meant to complement the front to create amazing effects. It shows real skills and is the mark of a good craftsperson, and it's beautiful.

But we're talking about cross stitch, where the canvas is thicker and the back isn't meant to be seen, so it can be stitched however you like and if it looks like a Jackson Pollack, maybe hang it that way around instead!

BACK IN BLACK

Let's do something crazy! Let's get our backs out! Back in Black (see page 34 for chart) can be stitched in whatever colour you like, but you have to hang it so that the question mark faces the other way.

So you cross stitch it as the pattern, but you hang it so people can see the back! And that's your art.

You can go monochrome if you want, or go gangbusters with colour and flair. Just make sure you show the back. Let's start a revolution.

I asked a bunch of my friends to stitch this design and show off their backs, and here's what we got (see right)!

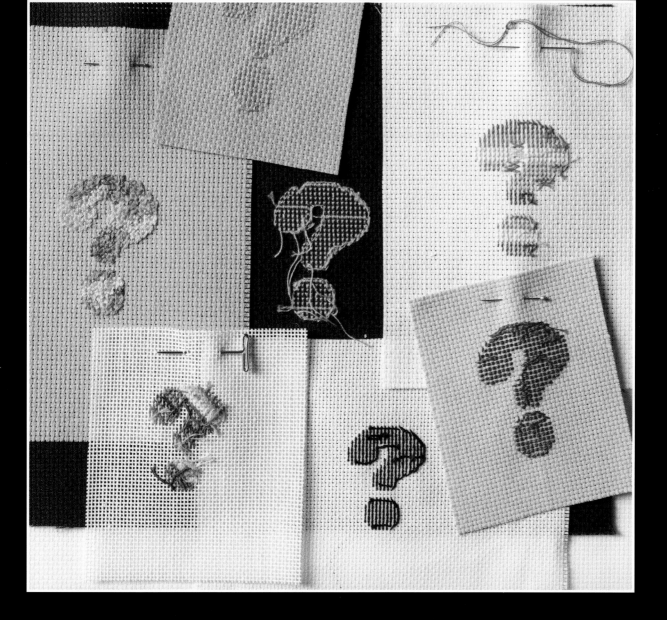

Here are some basic pointers that you can use to keep your back in check:

✗ If you are filling in a lighter colour and crossing areas that are already stitched in darker colours, consider wheedling the needle under some existing stitches to keep your thread tucked away. This process should also allow you to uncoil your thread.

✗ Every time you make a stitch, you put a half twist in the thread. After a while the thread will curl and gather on the rear as you pull your needle from back to front. This can lead to crazy knot shenanigans, which get worse when you've not noticed for a while. It's a good idea to drop the needle periodically and let the thread spin itself straight again. Then you can continue with less stress.

✗ Check the back of your work from time to time, to avoid stitching over those curly critters I mentioned earlier.

✗ If you do end up with a car crash on the back, fret not. If you're framing it in a hoop, place another piece of fabric over the back, before securing the frame, and it'll look tasty and tidy!

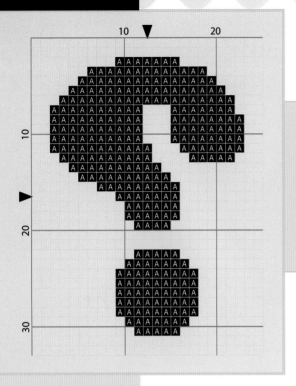

COLOUR KEY:

| A | ■ | 310 |

Design details
Difficulty: easy
Fabric count: 14
Width: 4.57cm (1¾in)
Height: 6.1cm (2⅜in)
Colours: up to you!
Stitches: 296

Hashtags:
#popart
#typography

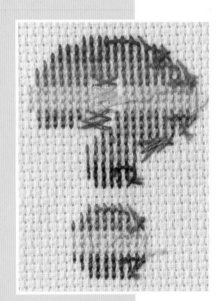

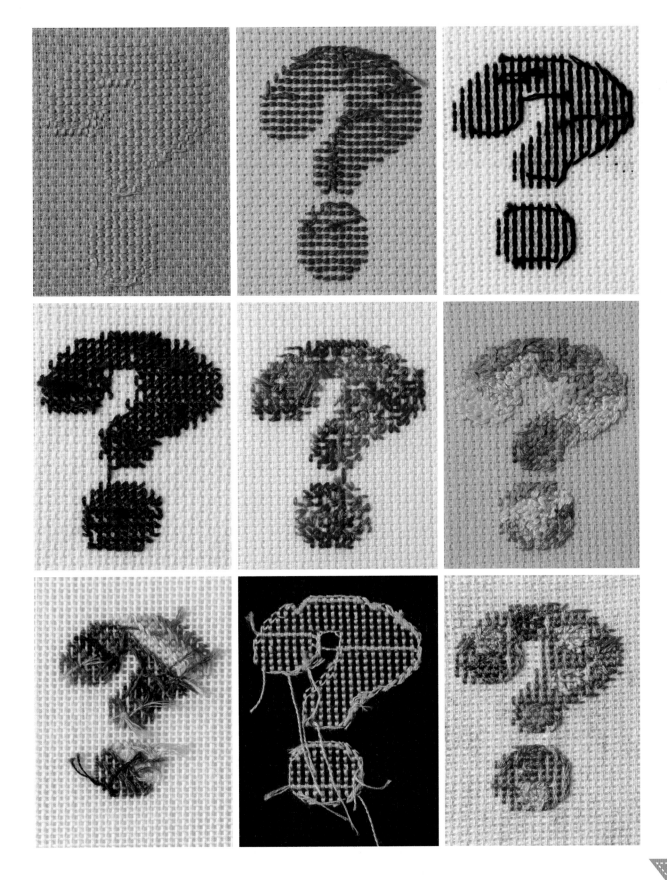

COLOUR

COLOUR

Colour, colour, everywhere and not a drop
to drink. Oh wait, that's not right...

We live in a colourful world and it's beautiful. It's created by light waves vibrating at different frequencies that interact with the light receptors in our eyes to illuminate our experience.

It is said that the human eye can distinguish about 10 million different colours, and when talking about physical colours, they can be plotted along an RYB – red, yellow, blue – spectrum. Printing uses a CMYK – cyan, magenta, yellow, black – spectrum as all colours can be printed using a combination of these colours.

There are three broad categories of colour, based on their composition:

✗ Primary: these are red, yellow and blue – the three colours that colour theory is based on
✗ Secondary: these are the combinations of primary colours:
  Red + Yellow = Orange
  Red + Blue = Purple
  Blue + Yellow = Green
✗ Tertiary: these are combinations of the primary and secondary colours that sit next to each other in a colour wheel, and include magenta (red-purple), teal (blue-green) and amber (yellow-orange).

You can create greys and browns by combining colours that are complementary and sit across from one another on the colour wheel – yellow + purple, for example.

Colour has three variables – hue, saturation and value:

✗ Hue is the colour of the colour
✗ Saturation is the intensity of the colour – from pale to vibrant
✗ Value is the strength of the colour – from light to dark.

There's a lot to be said about colour theory and Wikipedia is a good place to start learning. It's important to understand how the colours work together, be they in contrast or complement, when you're putting a design together. While beauty may be in the eye of the beholder, with a bit of time spent understanding the basic principles, you'll get a sense of what will or won't work, and you can design accordingly.

The good thing about the world of cross stitch is that the main thread manufacturers have done a good job of collating colour palettes that should give you the scheme you want, and there are plenty of online tools that can help you align other colours against those thread companies should you choose. So the world is your very colourful oyster!

FLEUR DE COULEUR

Years ago, I remember being struck by how vibrant a California poppy is in the sunlight. It's a remarkable colour and it sparked a casual interest in flowers with various attempts at growing them and keeping them alive over the years. I like dahlias in particular, with their diverse petal formations in a wild range of colour and size. They're ace.

I also appreciate a good flower arrangement. Now if any men were questioning the gender bias in a craft, I suspect that flower arranging can give cross stitch a run for its money.

If you've got nice flowers, it serves you well to spend a little time setting them up to look their best. But I digress.

Flowers and cross stitch have been firm friends even since the invention of cross stitch (or flowers, whichever came first) and if you're a fan of the floral, you'll find there's a ton of designs that'll make you happy.

I've taken the opportunity to combine a bit of floral with a basic colour wheel, showing the primary and secondary colours that exist within the spectrum. Here's some colour wheel pop art for ya. Stitch it on black and it'll look amazeballs.

Design details
Difficulty: medium
Fabric count: 14
Width: 15.25cm (6in)
Height: 15.25cm (6in)
Colours: 14
Stitches: 3,955

Hashtags:
#florals
#lifeiscolorful
#popart

FLEUR DE COULEUR CHART

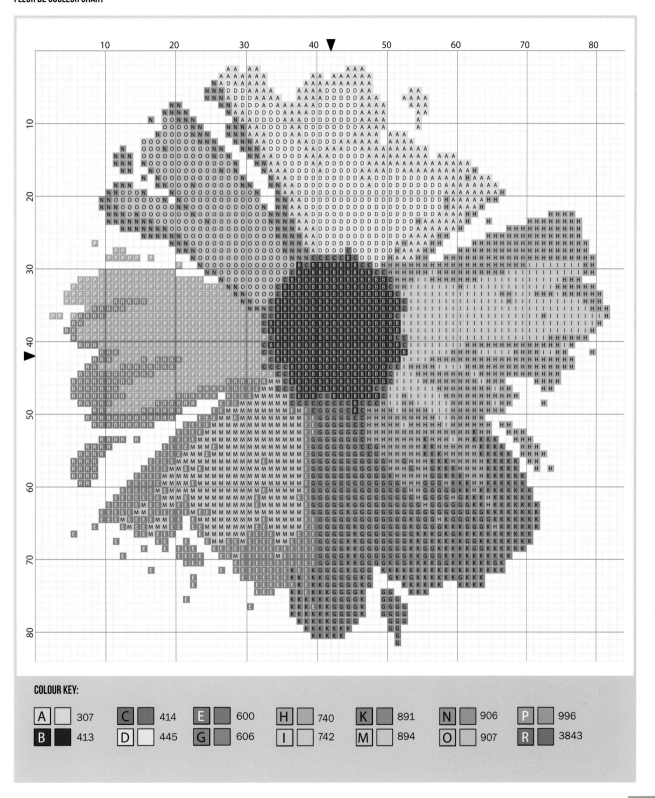

COLOUR KEY:

A 307	C 414	E 600	H 740	K 891	N 906	P 996
B 413	D 445	G 606	I 742	M 894	O 907	R 3843

FROM AMPERSAND TO BARGELLO

I like a good bit of typography. My grandfather was a typesetter for a newspaper and the shapes and forms of letters have always fascinated me. You'll find a few fonts at the back of the book that you can play around with (see pages 136–139), but here's a little something to get you going. I've taken two of my favourite design thingies and put them together – Ampersand and Bargello.

But what are Ampersand and Bargello? I hear you ask! Ladies and gentlemen, it's Wikipedia:

"The word ampersand is a corruption of the phrase 'and per se & (and)', meaning 'and intrinsically the word and (represented by the symbol &)'. The ampersand can be traced back to the 1st century AD and the Old Roman cursive, in which the letters E and T occasionally were written together to form a ligature."

en.wikipedia.org/wiki/Ampersand

Wikipedia defines Bargello as follows:

"Bargello is a type of needlepoint embroidery consisting of upright flat stitches laid in a mathematical pattern to create motifs. The name originates from a series of chairs found in the Bargello palace in Florence, which have a 'flame stitch' pattern.
Traditionally, Bargello was stitched in wool on canvas. Embroidery done this way is remarkably durable. It is well suited for use on pillows, upholstery and even carpets, but not for clothing. In most traditional pieces, all stitches are vertical with stitches going over two or more threads.
Traditional designs are very colourful, and use many hues of one colour, which produces intricate shading effects. The patterns are naturally geometric, but can also resemble very stylised flowers or fruits. Bargello is considered particularly challenging, as it requires very precise counting of squares for the mathematical pattern connected with the various motifs to accurately execute designs."

en.wikipedia.org/wiki/Bargello_(needlework)

So there you have it. Here's a bit of Bargello for you. And?

Design details
Difficulty: easy
Fabric count: 14
Width: 14cm (5½in)
Height: 11cm (4¼in)
Colours: 10
Stitches: 4,484

Hashtags:
#bargello
#lifeiscolorful
#typography

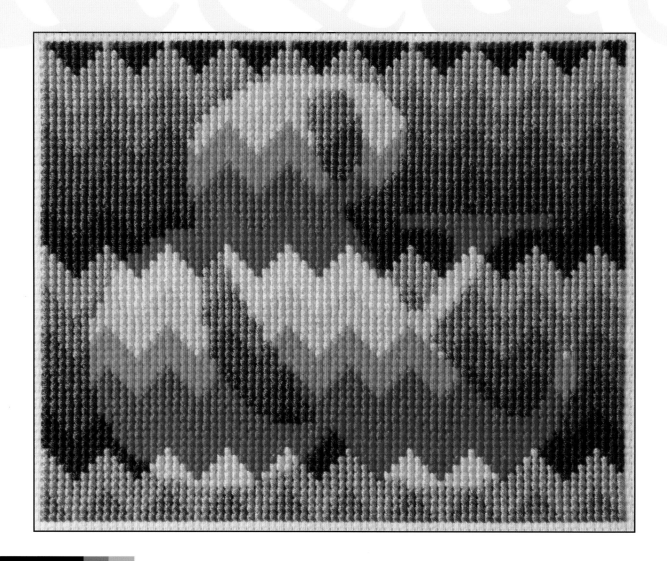

COLOUR KEY:

A	307	C	645	E	647	H	666	K	900
B	444	D	646	G	648	I	844	M	947

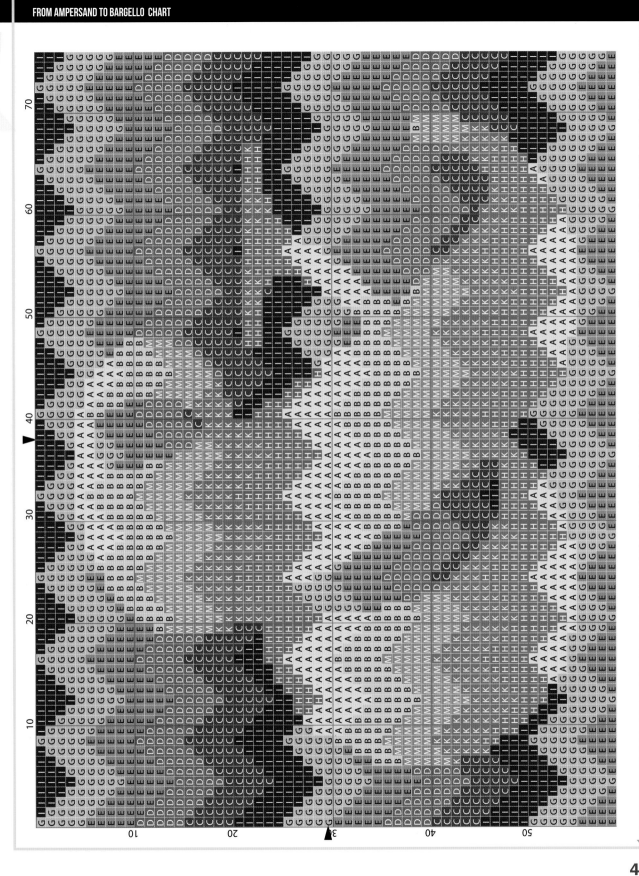

A MOMENT OF CONTEXT

By doing cross stitch you are taking part in a cultural craft that spans generations and continents. In 2009 at the Kostyonki excavation site in Russia, they found ivory needles that were dated to 30,000 years ago. Yes, that's right, thirty thousand years ago! Now I love social media, but that's been around a decade at most, and cinema has been around for 200 years tops. But embroidery has been around for millennia.

Some of the world's most precious historical events are immortalised in stitch, from the Bayeux Tapestry to the Great Tapestry of Scotland. Cross stitch samplers were commonly used as a way of teaching embroidery, and the crafter would literally pinpoint their place in space and time among the flowery borders and earnest phrases.

It feels like the traditional sampler has somewhat fallen by the wayside – aside from the very traditional style, the odd Cthulhu mashup is the closest I've seen to a fresh take on this old classic. However, many people take the time to share wisdom and thoughtful phrases via the medium of embroidery and cross stitch, and they make the world a better place by doing so.

Cross stitch is a global craft, popular throughout the world and whether you're in South America or Eastern Europe, you won't have to look far to find some stitching. Different countries have different tastes in cross stitch, but the passion and the benefits gained from this humble needlecraft have inspired generations of stitchers across the years and across the world.

The process of stitching is a profound one, more on that later, but it's also a time-consuming one, so you don't want to waste too much time stitching things of little relevance. You want to capture the words of others and use them to inspire others. You want to stitch something meaningful.

SOMETHING MEANINGFUL

Pretty deep, huh? As well as being massively thought-provoking [cough], this pattern gives you a chance to use the most cowboy of all colour schemes – ombré.

Colour graduation can give a nice sense of flow and movement in an otherwise static image, and if you bust out the backstitch, you can have some real fun with it. Don't feel constrained by the pinks I've thrown at you – choose six colours that you think will transition nicely and go for it!

The brush font created for this design was inspired by hundreds of similar fonts on the internet. If you're a font geek, 1001freefonts.com is a great site to meander through. The good news is that this font and a few others are located at the back of the book (see pages 136–139), so you can stitch whatever you fancy!

Design details
Difficulty: easy
Fabric count: 14
Width: 21.5cm (8½in)
Height: 11cm (4¼in)
Colours: 6
Stitches: 1,637

Hashtags:
#ombre
#typography
#zen

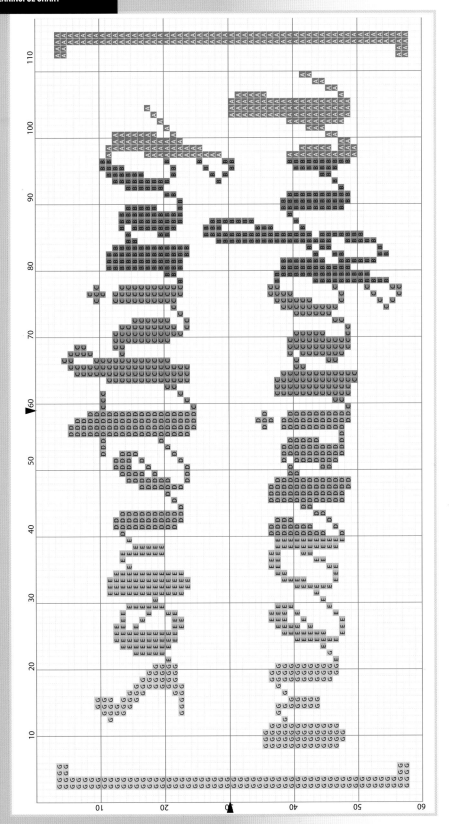

COLOUR KEY:

A		600
B		601
C		602
D		603
E		604
G		605

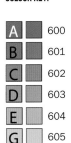

SQRL!

Check out this guy. He's a chirpy little fella! Keep an eye on your wallet if you're spending too much time near him – he's a bit nuts!

SQRL features the very groovy geometric approach to design, and in cross stitch terms that means it's time to bust out the three-quarter stitch! Alongside its humble associate the quarter stitch, the three-quarter stitch is a great way of getting some sharp angles in whatever you're designing.

The three-quarter stitch is pretty straightforward, as you simply wheedle your needle through the centre of the square you're stitching, and pull the thread through. This creates a quarter stitch, which is followed by a full stitch along the required diagonal for the effect.

SQRL's quite the angular little critter, so by the time he's stitched up and ready to go, you should be proficient in three-quarter and quarter stitches and ready to go-go geometry!

Design details
Difficulty: hard
Fabric count: 14
Width: 14cm (5½in)
Height: 19.8cm (7¾in)
Colours: 12
Stitches: 5,034

Hashtags:
#geometry
#threequarterstitch
#wildlife

1 We can see a finished three-quarter stitch with our orange friend here. To make one, come up at the point you want as the epicentre of the stitch, but instead of going to the diagonally opposite hole...

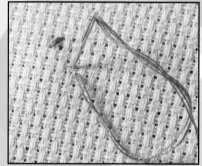

2 ...wheedle your needle through the centre of the Aida weave in the middle of the square and pull through.

3 This creates the quarter stitch, which becomes a three-quarter stitch once you've added the extra diagonal stitch across. Sometimes you'll just want a quarter stitch to finish off a square and now you can see how easy those are to make!

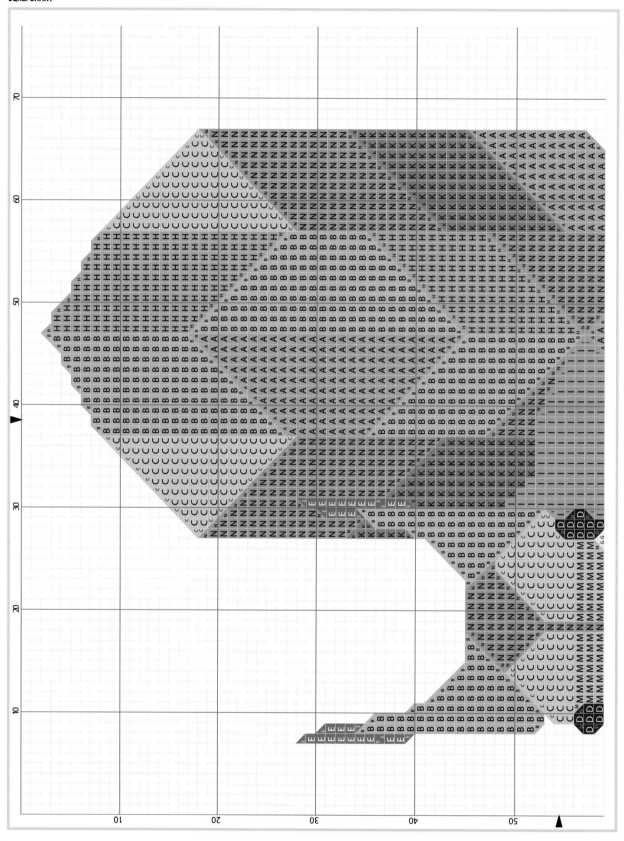

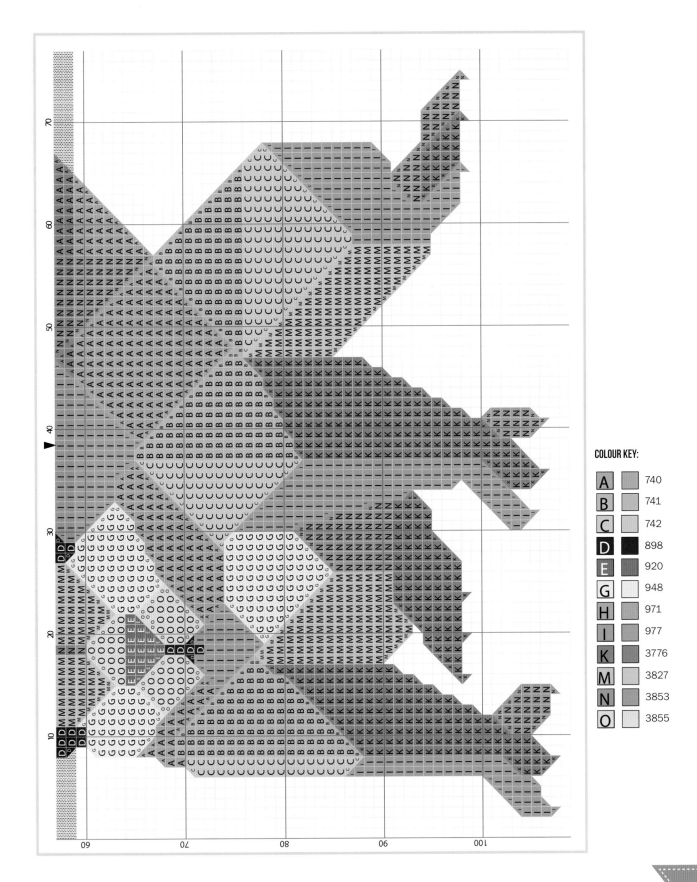

COLOUR KEY:

A		740
B		741
C		742
D		898
E		920
G		948
H		971
I		977
K		3776
M		3827
N		3853
O		3855

OUTLIER: ZOE GILBERTSON

Colour
Zoe Gilbertson combines abstract aspects and clever colour combinations to create cross stitch designs with pixel perfection.

1 When did you first start stitching and how did you find it?

I started stitching about eight years ago when I was asked to join a craft-and-wine type group with friends. I'm not really a 'crafty' person so I didn't know what to do with myself while they were knitting or paper-making or whatever. I'd seen an interesting needlepoint cushion in a local tapestry shop and thought I'd have a go at something similar. Sue in the shop gave me a few tips and off I went and copied a Venetian Bargello design. You can relax and talk (and drink wine) while stitching, so it worked for me! From then on I was hooked and immediately started working out abstract designs and ways to make time-consuming pieces become art. As a clothing designer by background, I'm lucky that I had the confidence, if not the skills, to design my own work and just get on with it.

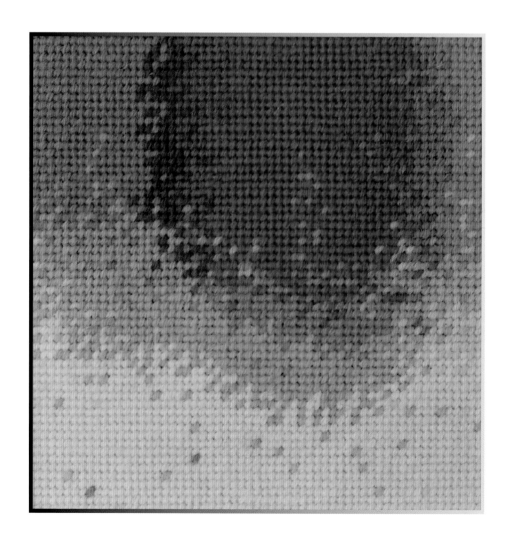

2 How do you create your designs?

I create designs in a variety of ways, it's always changing. Sometimes they are days in the planning; they might start as a drawing or painting, or I might design something in Adobe Illustrator then import it into MacStitch (a stitch program) and work on it there. I like exploring the effects of importing digital images from one program to another – sometimes it produces startling results. Sometimes I go straight to the canvas without having anything but a few vague thoughts in mind. I'm always trying different ways to recreate what's in the back of my mind. My current piece was planned and measured on a piece of paper, which I place under the canvas as a starting reference. I also usually mark the edge of the canvas with a marker pen every 10 lines so I know where I am.

3 Colour and abstraction are strong themes in your work. Can you tell me more about that?

A teacher wrote in my school report when I was four "Zoe has an eye for colour". I'm always drawn to playing with colour, particularly complements and contrasts. I'm rarely happy with what I do though, so I'm always striving to find something better. I think it might be a never-ending quest as the fashion designer in me is always looking for the next thing. I work with abstract themes at the moment, but I often consider more literal themes; they just haven't got anywhere yet. I think that's because I'm drawn to abstract, modernist, contemporary art and it's what I'm trying to create. I want to create art that I can put on my own wall and be proud of. I'm not sure I'm there yet.

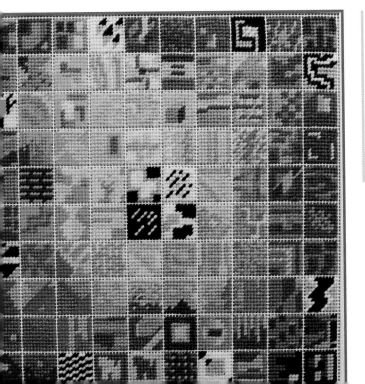

4 The process of cross stitch can be meditative and soothing – do you have any thoughts on this?

I don't actually find cross stitch calming – that's why I stick to tent stitch or Bargello styles of stitching. A single process stitch suits my brain! I do, however, find that I get anxious if I'm sitting doing nothing and I don't have any stitching with me. It's certainly calming when I do it. I usually stitch at the end of the day in front of the TV when the kids are in bed. It's a real treat and I don't tend to do it during the day. I don't want it to start to feel like work and I want to keep it precious.

GLOW IN THE DARK

GLOW IN THE DARK

Much underused, but capable of so many great illusions, glow-in-the-dark thread might become your new best friend!

GLOW-IN-THE-DARK THREAD

I don't really understand why glow-in-the-dark (GitD) thread isn't widely used within cross stitch as it's one of the most fun thread types to play with. GitD threads are coated with a phosphorous substance that absorbs light and emits it over a period of time. Innovations in technology mean that modern threads will hang on to the glow for longer than they used to and they are also quite resistant to washing.

There aren't many GitD products on the market but most manufacturers have a version of it. Kreinik have a wide range of GitD threads including filaments that you can combine with other threads to funk things up a little bit. You can also buy GitD fabric paints and there's an emerging market in GitD fabric as well, so there is an increasing number of possibilities of what you can do to show off your fluorescent flair!

Generally speaking, GitD thread will be off-white in colour, and will glow green when it's charged. The longevity of the glow will vary, and I wouldn't expect your stitches to be glowing all night long, but you can still have a bit of fun with them.

A quick note about how the patterns in this section work. Because GitD thread is off-white, it's tricky to see the effect in these designs, so for each pattern I've replaced it with DMC 600 (Cranberry) to show where the GitD should be.

Without further ado, on your marks, get set, glow!

EMPIRE STATE

If you like a good city, I don't think you can beat New York. People might think London's good, but it doesn't have the same sense of awe that you get from the skyscrapers of NYC, and the vibrant hustle and bustle of the city is intoxicating. Big shout out to the Brooklyn massive as well, for being an epicentre for needlecrafts and keeping the craft alive way before the hipsters started paying attention.

There are a million things to do in New York, but if I can offer one tip to the new visitor it's that you should enjoy the NYC skyline from the top of the Rockefeller Centre, rather than going to the top of the Empire State Building. That way, you can see the Empire State Building in all its glory, and it's a great sight.

Design details
Difficulty: medium
Fabric count: 14
Width: 15.25cm (6in)
Height: 20.3cm (8in)
Colours: 13
Stitches: 4,523

Hashtags:
#backstitch
#glowinthedark
#landscape
#threequarterstitch

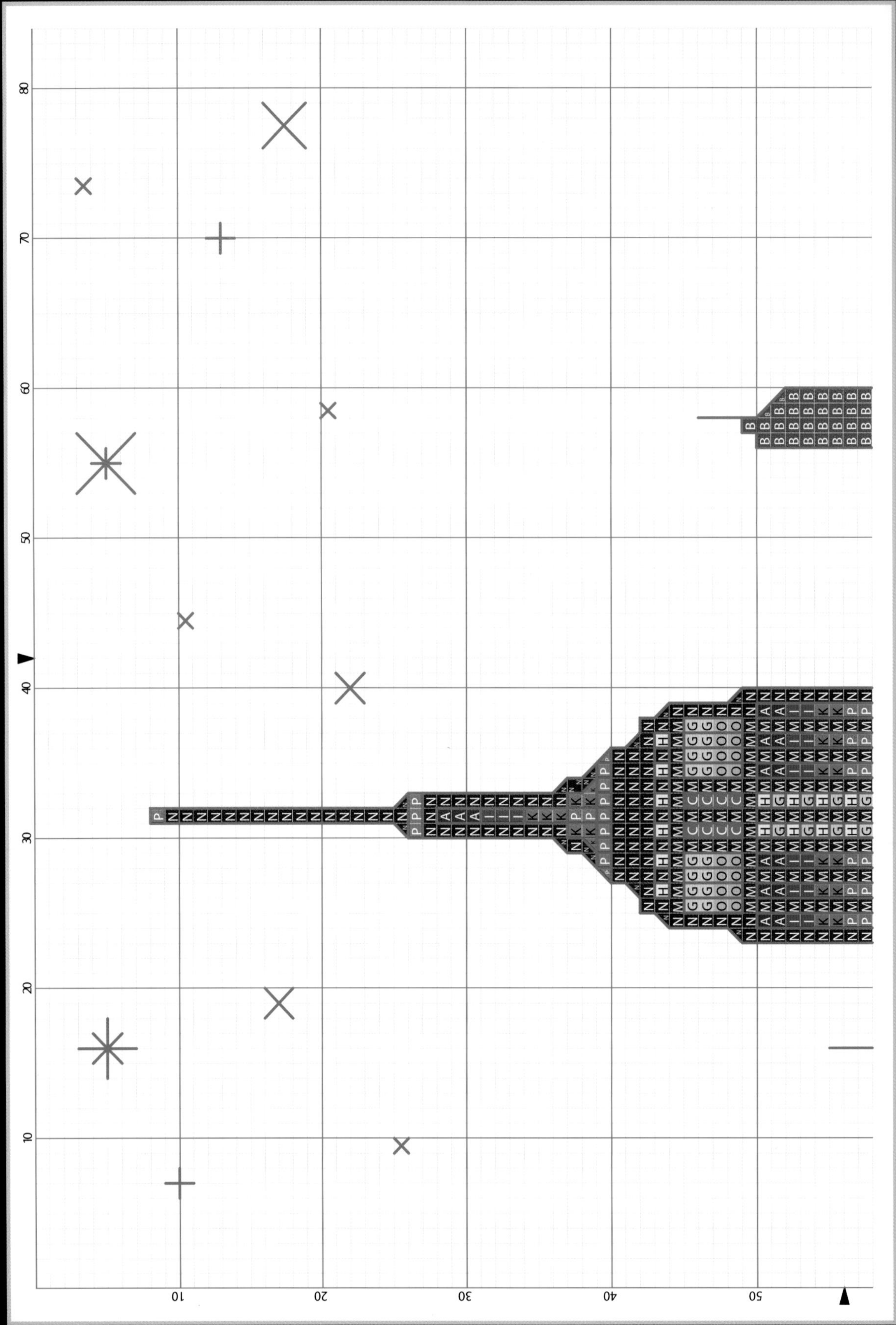

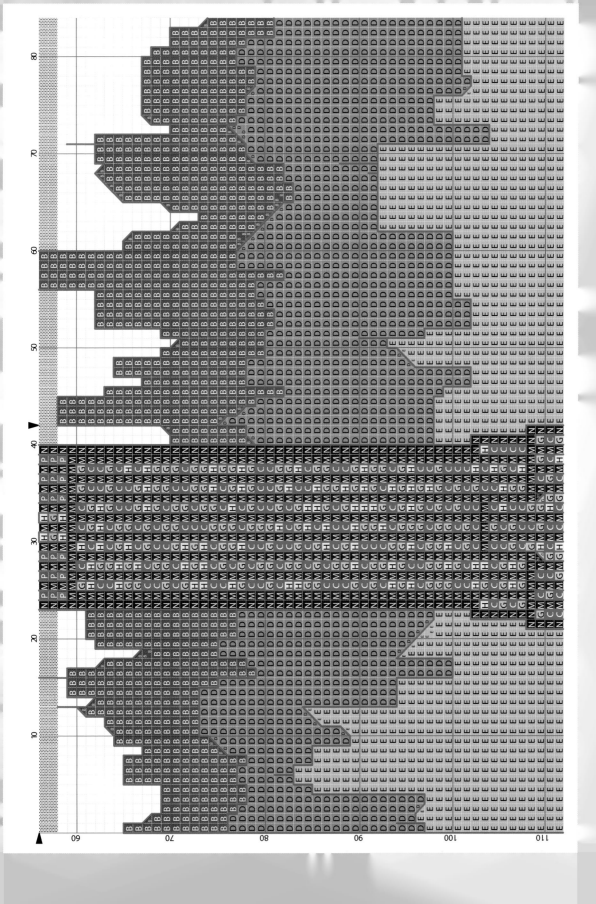

COLOUR KEY:

A		158	D		647	H		762	M		844	P	3843
B		317	E		648	I		798	N		3799		
C		600	G		725	K		826	O		3820		

Backstitch lines:
——————— 600

NB: Cranberry 600 represents GitD thread E940.

STITCHING AND TRAVELLING

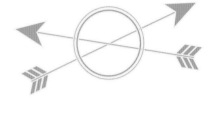

I love to take some stitching with me when I go travelling, as it's the ideal pastime while on a long flight or train journey. Not only is it light and easy to carry, it's far more interesting than staring out of the window or reading something on your phone, let alone talking to a stranger (the horror!).

I'd like to clear something up straight away – it's okay to take needles on planes, and you can take scissors as long as the blade length is less than 4cm (1½in). If in doubt, get a thread cutter and it negates the whole argument.

   I have a handy little fabric pouch that I use to carry needles, threads and a cutter of some sort. Here are some observations I've made over the years of stitching in public and while travelling:

- ✗ If you want a bit of space to yourself on a train, be a bald man doing cross stitch and you'll find that no one sits near you unless there's no other choice.

- ✗ Sometimes people will ask you what you're doing, but I suspect it helps to be friendly looking while you're stitching. My concentration frown can be misinterpreted, so I don't get chatting that often, but I'm sure that's as much a reflection of English train journeys – know what I mean, English people?

- ✗ If you're on a flight, it doesn't hurt to let the flight attendants see what you're doing, as it'll make you marginally more interesting than the average. This, in turn, can improve your gin and tonic refill rate, if you play your cards right.

- ✗ Stitching on subways or underground trains is good training for getting the needle to stitch exactly where you want. Anyone who can stitch on black fabric on a tube train that's bouncing around all over the place can consider themselves a fearsome needlecraft ninja.

- ✗ The same can be said for stitching on horseback – just avoid using your steed as a pincushion.

- ✗ It never hurts to carry some extra thread and fabric with you when travelling, as you might convert a fellow passenger. Don't try to force it on people though.

- ✗ Take plenty of needles as it's a bugger trying to get your last one out of the crevice of a plane seat.

Remember that if you choose to stitch while travelling, you're an ambassador for one of the world's oldest crafts, so be sure to act with the necessary respect.

WINTER IS COMING

It is fair to say that the world of geekcraft has never been healthier.

Whether it's cosplay, weapon building or the myriad of handcrafts inspired by pop culture, thanks to sites such as DeviantArt you can find all manner of homemade homages to our favourite books, shows and films.

I'll talk about sci-fi later in the book, but I thought I'd take a moment to give a nod to one of the best TV shows to have happened in recent years – *Game of Thrones*. Full confession, dear readers, I resisted watching *GoT* for a very long time, but I relented when the fifth series came out and I'm glad I did, as it truly is an epic tale of love and loss.

From the second series onwards, it became clear that *GoT* was becoming a fan favourite, and this was reflected in the craft world with an explosion in cross stitched references and textile mashups. If you look hard enough at the programme you'll catch glimpses of the work of Michele Carragher, the *GoT* lead embroiderer who has produced all manner of stunning hand-embellished outfits for the main characters, many of whom are promptly killed while wearing them.

Whether it's *The Lord of The Rings*, *Harry Potter* or *The Dark Crystal*, you'll find thousands of stitchers that have been inspired to share their allegiances and honour their heroes. Winter is Coming is my addition to the mix, and I've experimented with glow-in-the-dark thread to produce a dual-effect piece.

Stitch it on black fabric for the best effect; the outline of the text and the stitches that appear grey in the image should be stitched in GitD, so that by day it looks like Winter is Coming, but at night we see that Winter is Here and, well, we'd better keep our eyes peeled for the Night King and his White Walker army, hadn't we?

With this design, make sure that you backstitch the word 'Coming' in white, rather than GitD!

Design details
Difficulty: medium
Fabric count: 14
Width: 19cm (7½in)
Height: 18cm (7in)
Colours: 4
Stitches: 5,001

Hashtags:
#backstitch
#geekcraft
#glowinthedark

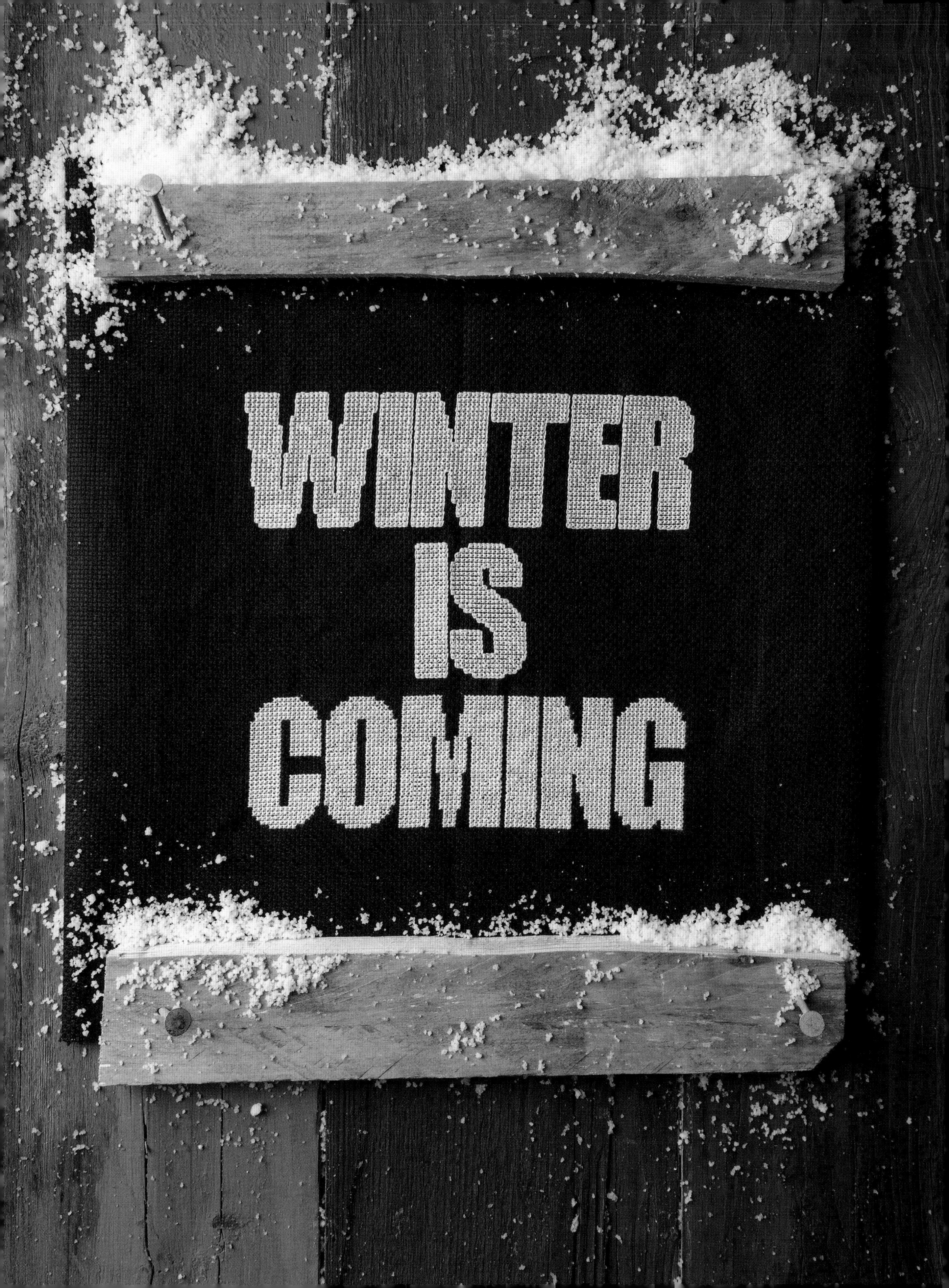
WINTER
IS
COMING

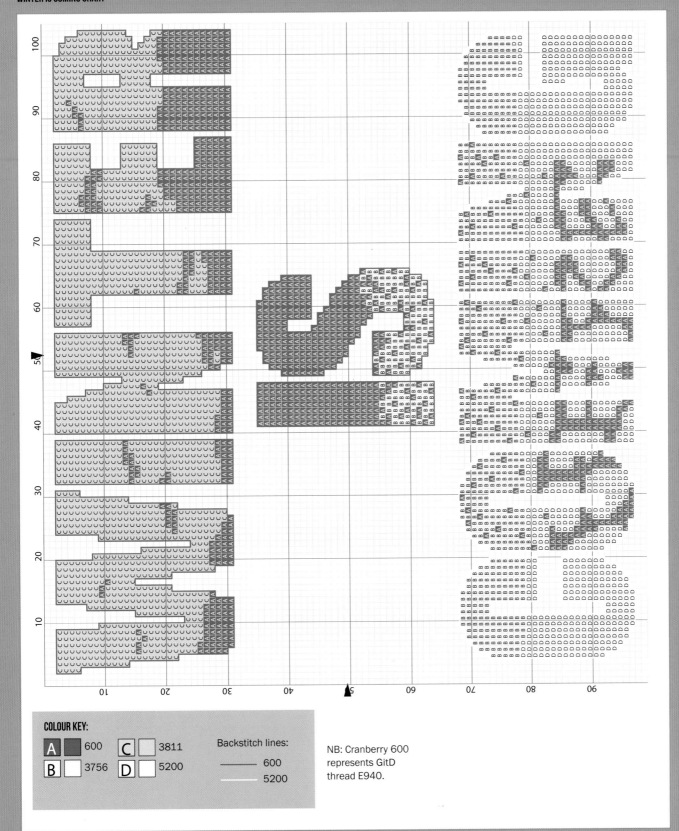

COLOUR KEY:

A	600	C	3811
B	3756	D	5200

Backstitch lines:

——— 600

——— 5200

NB: Cranberry 600 represents GitD thread E940.

VODKATOMIC

Back in the day, whenever I cut off a bit of excess thread, rather than throwing it on the floor, I'd eat it. I can't really explain why the notion of putting it in the bin wasn't part of the equation, but anyway... not something I'd recommend! Once I started tinkering with GitD I decided that my eating strategy ought to end, lest I end up with a glow-in-the-dark belly! Of course, had I been around in the 1950s, I'd have been encouraged to try atomic options and I'm sure that a VodkAtomic would have been the drink of choice. I'll have mine irradiated, not stirred!

Design details
Difficulty: medium
Fabric count: 14
Width: 14cm (5½in)
Height: 17.8cm (7in)
Colours: 14
Stitches: 2,781

VODKATOMIC CHART

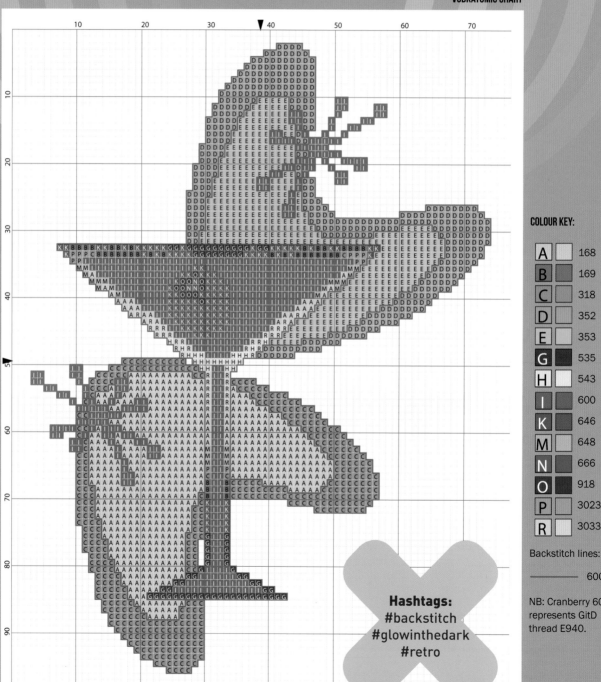

COLOUR KEY:

A		168
B		169
C		318
D		352
E		353
G		535
H		543
I		600
K		646
M		648
N		666
O		918
P		3023
R		3033

Backstitch lines:

——— 600

NB: Cranberry 600 represents GitD thread E940.

Hashtags:
#backstitch
#glowinthedark
#retro

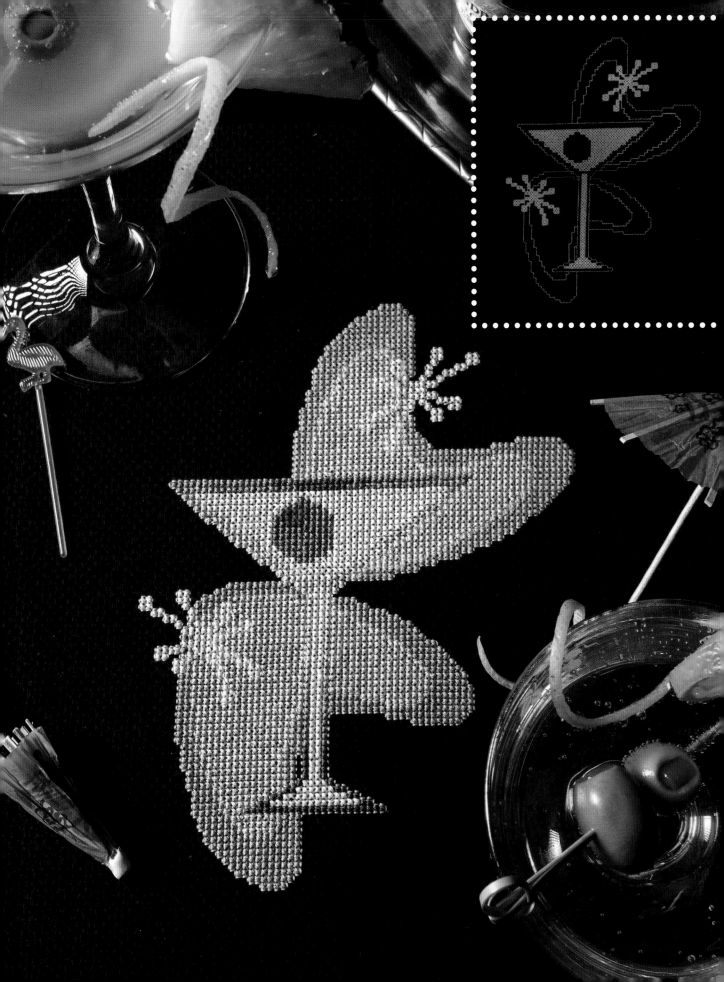

OUTLIER: KATE BLANDFORD

1 When did you first start stitching and how did you find it?

My first cross stitch was a freebie my mum got with one of her magazines. I couldn't have been any older than about eight. It was a little white house with a flowery trellis on the front. It was one of those kits that once you finished stitching it you could put it in a card and send it to your nan. It was pretty naff to be fair.

I have always been surrounded by textiles, thanks to my mum. She used to make me and my brother the most gnarly knitted '80s/'90s film and TV icon sweatshirts. I didn't know anyone else with a pink Teenage Mutant Ninja Turtles sweater. From a young age I knew craft could be cool.

Roll on ten years and I managed to bag a space at Goldsmiths [part of the University of London] to study textiles. Embroidery was something I was always inspired by but didn't practise often, that is until I started my MA in graphic arts three years later. I started to tap into it in a way that made sense to me. I found a lot of the stuff being churned out on my course a bit soulless. I wasn't ready to give up my Blue Peter childhood in favour of a future in computer wizardry.

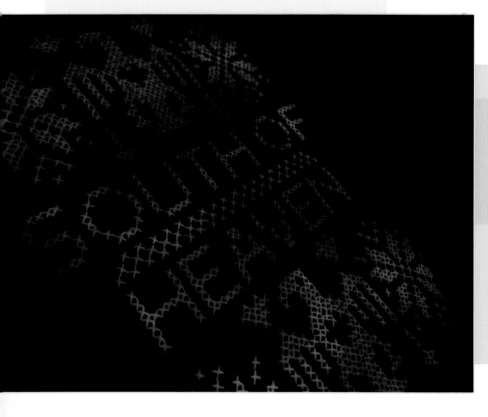

To me, embroidery had meaning. It was nostalgic. It showed skill, time and dedication. Sometimes it made people laugh. I loved the tactility of it all. I liked that it physically existed and could incite emotion and memories more than anything I could ever produce on a computer screen. I played around with a lot of digital cross stitch stuff but nothing can compare to the real McCoy.

2 What do you enjoy about working with GitD thread?

The best thing about GitD thread is the surprise element. I use DMC Light Effects in my pieces, which looks just like any other white thread... that is, until someone hits the lights.

It's fun, you can shake it up and use with regular white thread to sneak in hidden motifs or text around the stitches that glow – think of it as a bit of a contemporary twist on traditional Assisi embroidery.

It can be a bit of a beast to tame – I've learned that cutting shorter pieces of thread makes it more manageable and less prone to fraying. Thread conditioner wouldn't go amiss either!

3 You've also been known to stitch outside the hoop – tell me about that.

I've never been one for convention. Being outside the hoop means you can really explore the world around you. It's pretty liberating and I urge everyone to give it a go!

I'm constantly on the look out for things I can stitch into. Previously anything with multiple holes was fair game. Now with water soluble canvas and laser cutters easier to come by, anything is possible. Not being confined to a hoop means you can really push the materials that you use and come up with some pretty interesting pieces that can totally challenge people's perceptions of cross stitch.

4 The process of cross stitch can be meditative and soothing – do you have any thoughts on this?

I can quite often find myself stitching for hours and wondering where the day has gone. Getting lost in a piece and escaping from the day-to-day stresses of life is always good. Also, there's definitely something cathartic about stabbing material a hundred times after a particularly taxing day.

5 You're renowned for your heavy metal approach to embroidery – what inspires you?

Someone once called me "shabby chic for satanists" and I really thought they hit the nail on the head. I love alternative music and I'm a sucker for a good pattern. Why not fuse two loves together?

MORE THAN A HOBBY

MORE THAN A HOBBY

It might seem like a simple needlecraft, but cross stitch is far more profound than you might realise.

PEACE OF MIND

We live in a very hectic world, with all kinds of stresses and strains coming at us from all angles. If we're lucky, we've got a roof over our heads, food in our bellies and our main worries are Fear of Missing Out and Keeping Up With the Kardashians. If we're unlucky – well, there are thousands of effects of modern life that can harm us, and it's often up to us to find the resilience to overcome them.

However, us human beings are blessed with higher brain functions that can help us deal with life's curve balls and the concept of mindfulness has been cited as a great way of tapping into these functions.

Wikipedia describes mindfulness as:

> "the psychological process of bringing one's attention to the internal and external experiences occurring in the present moment, which can be developed through the practice of meditation and other training... Large population-based research studies have indicated that the practice of mindfulness is strongly correlated with wellbeing and perceived health. Studies have also shown that rumination and worry contribute to mental illnesses such as depression and anxiety, and that mindfulness-based interventions are effective in the reduction of both rumination and worry."

en.wikipedia.org/wiki/Mindfulness

I GOT YER MINDFULNESS RIGHT HERE

Pretty awesome, huh? Now, if there's one thing we can say for sure about cross stitch, it's that it focuses your attention on the present moment, as you take time to make sure your stitching goes the way you want. In those moments, when you're not thinking about the day's events, or what the future has to hold, you're just sitting in the present, existing in a state of mindfulness. In those moments, you're at peace.

So there. You want mindfulness..?

This mindfulness pattern not only gives us a vibrant rainbow of colour to enjoy stitching, and an opportunity to see how we feel about the different colour frequencies in front of us, but I've busted out the backstitch to create one of my favourite 3D effects. Pay attention to those diagonals as they change to create the illusion of grandeur.

Design details
Difficulty: easy
Fabric count: 14
Width: 23cm (9in)
Height: 7.5cm (3in)
Colours: 12
Stitches: 1,062

Hashtags:
#backstitch
#lifeiscolorful
#ombre
#3D
#typography

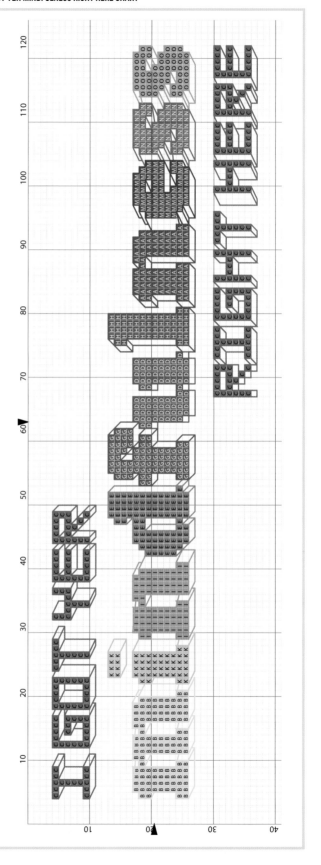

COLOUR KEY:

A		208
B		307
C		414
D		600
K		742
M		798
N		3843
O		3846

E		608
G		666
H		718
I		740

Backstitch lines:

—————— 208
—————— 307
—————— 414
—————— 600

—————— 608
—————— 666
—————— 718
—————— 740

—————— 742
—————— 798
—————— 3843
—————— 3846

EMBROIDERY AS THERAPY

Most of us know that crafts make us feel good. With a bit of luck the process of making is relatively pain free, and there's a great sense of satisfaction to be gained from completing a piece and giving it to someone special.

However, anyone who's tried a craft and stuck with it for a while will realise that there's something profoundly soothing about the combination of mindfulness and creativity. It's hard to explain, but I have taught many, many cross stitch workshops and I always enjoy when, about half an hour in, people have overcome the learning curve and are settling into that space. You can tell they're getting a warm, fuzzy feeling that emanates from within, and that's the magic.

Although the evidence is scarce, there's an increasing amount of research into the positive benefits of craft on mental health and wellbeing. A 2013 study by Dr Jill Riley from Cardiff University interviewed more than 3,500 knitters and concluded that:

"Knitting has significant psychological and social benefits, which can contribute to wellbeing and quality of life. As a skilled and creative occupation, it has therapeutic potential..."

(bjo.sagepub.com/content/76/2/50.abstract)

The results showed that knitters felt happier and calmer after a session with the needles, and that there was some evidence of higher cognitive functioning among frequent knitters. In other words, the process of crafting not only soothed people, but it kept their brains sharper as well!

On top of that, neuroscientists suggest that repetitive motions engage the same nervous systems that relate to the fight-or-flight responses, easing pressure on those systems and helping us manage moderate stress. While we might not need to flee from death in the same way as our biological ancestors thousands of years ago, the same systems exist within us and process our anxieties; anything that alleviates that tension is a good thing.

For many people the pleasure of completion and the consequential rise in self-efficacy – how we feel about performing tasks – is also a critical part of their wellbeing, and a simple way to diffuse fear of failure when getting things done. If you can finish a cross stitch, you're able to finish other things, and so it goes.

Lastly, there's a school of thought that suggests that handcrafts can lead to the production of dopamine, the feelgood chemical, in our brains. What's not to love?

As the modern world continues to barrage us with stresses and strains, it's important to realise that cross stitch (as well as most other handcrafts) can bring us pleasure on a number of levels and can actually be used as a tool for positive development and boosting your sense of wellbeing.

As I always say, don't get angry – get cross (stitch)!

I AM AN ADDICT

Addiction is no laughing matter, unless you're addicted to laughing. Most of us will have gotten hooked on something at some point and, if we're unlucky, we have to fight that addiction to loosen its hold.

Sometimes it's just a question of going cold turkey and waiting for time to pass while the addiction fades, and in times like that, it's good to have something to do. Like embroidery.

You can use this pattern to pass the time and while you're doing it, you can ponder on the nature of your addiction (if you have one) and envisage it fading away, like this nifty little blackwork design. Alternatively, if the only addiction you've got is for cross stitch, then celebrate that fact and get this backstitch bad boy up on your wall!

Blackwork

Blackwork is a form of embroidery that dates back to at least the 15th century, if not earlier. In essence, it uses running stitch and backstitch to create linework forms and patterns.

By manipulating the density of stitches in the pattern or the number of threads, the appearance of depth and texture can be created.

Traditionally, blackwork is done with black threads, as redwork is done with red, but the term 'blackwork' is more commonly applied to the design principles rather than the colour of the thread.

Not all black work is blackwork.

Design details
Difficulty: hard
Fabric count: 18
Width: 15.25cm (6in)
Height: 7cm (2¾in)
Colours: 3
Stitches: 333
(backstitch)

Hashtags:
#backstitch
#ombre
#3D
#typography
#zen

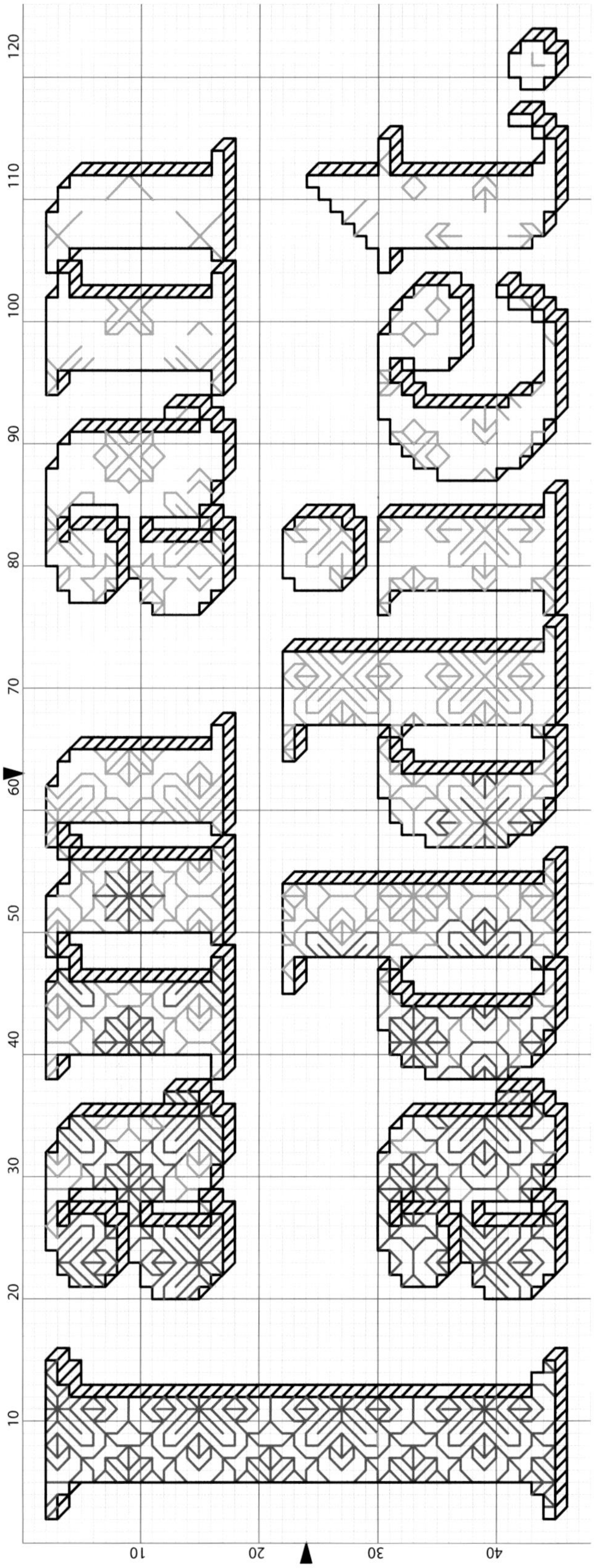

Note: colour 3705 is actually red, but is shown on the chart as blue to distinguish it from 321.

COLOUR KEY:

Backstitch lines:

— 310

— 321

— 3705

CRAFTIVISM

If you're concerned with the way of the world and you'd like to make a statement about it, craftivism provides a gentle way to express your feelings. The phrase was originally coined by Betsy Greer, who brought the concepts of craft and activism together to reflect a new form of political expression: "Craftivism to me is a way of looking at life where voicing opinions through creativity makes your voice stronger, your compassion deeper & your quest for justice more infinite."

craftingagreenworld.com/2009/04/04/what-is-craftivism-division-over-the-definition-explodes-an-etsy-team/

Design details
Difficulty: easy
Fabric count: 14
Width: 17.53cm (6⅞in)
Height: 17.27cm (6¾in)
Colours: 9
Stitches: 3,465

Hashtags:
#craftivism
#lifeiscolorful
#stitchforsyria

Understandably for some people, the idea of carrying a placard around in protest over a specific issue is a bit too much to ask, so craftivism allows people the means to critically explore issues using handcrafts, and often embroidery, as a medium.

Sarah Corbett founded the Craftivist Collective (craftivist-collective.com) in 2009 and has led a wide range of campaigns looking at the consequences of globalisation, and using embroidery as the medium of expression. One of the recent campaigns – #imapiece – involved the creation of hand-embroidered jigsaw pieces that provided solutions to many of the challenges of the modern world and inspired over 500 people to participate. Sarah encourages craftivists to use the time spent creating their work as an opportunity for reflecting on the subject they're stitching, to know and feel their responses. As we've noted with the mindfulness concept, this level of considered creation is hugely powerful and is a great tool for change.

One of the most amazing aspects of craftivism is the effect that handmade items have on decision makers. People intrinsically understand how long a cross stitch can take and it drives the message home harder than a simple email ever could. So if you're feeling passionate about an issue, but don't think that a letter to an MP is going to make a difference, pick up a needle and become a craftivist – the power is within you.

#STITCHFORSYRIA

In 2015 I was invited to work with Concern Worldwide on a craftivism project, and #stitchforsyria was born. I asked the team at Concern to tell you about it, so here goes:

In early 2016 Concern Worldwide (a humanitarian and development charity) launched Stitch for Syria. They invited their supporters to take on a cross stitch challenge to show support for a group of female Syrian refugees in Lebanon, who are using cross stitch to earn a vital income and deal with the trauma of all they have been through.

The organisation knew that the UK public cared deeply about the Syria crisis, and wanted to help. But this was about much more than spending two minutes signing a petition or forwarding an email – they wanted supporters to spend hours working away with a needle and thread. They were asking stitchers to make a section of a wall hanging for the centre in Lebanon where the women meet, as a message of support and solidarity.

The charity needed to convince people just how important the craft sessions were to the refugees. So they let the refugees themselves explain why the project is so important. Yesenia* said: "It's the one time of day when I can forget my problems and focus on something good." Yara* told us: "The teachers and the friends I have made have become like family, a reason to keep going."

Hundreds of people quickly downloaded the beautiful pattern, which is based on a traditional Middle Eastern design. The charity received completed works from every corner of the UK as well as 19 other countries. The amazing sense of community shared by cross stitchers around the world was at the heart of the campaign. Every time there were pictures shared on social media of a group sitting around a table stitching together – just like the women at the project in Lebanon – you could see the campaign was working.

The stitches came thick and fast – Concern received more than 800 completed patterns. And while most people were happy to keep things simple, a few couldn't resist putting their own twist on the design. These ranged from neon thread and video game references to beads, borders and more funky extras.

*names have been changed

COLOUR KEY:

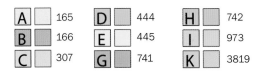

A	165	D	444	H	742
B	166	E	445	I	973
C	307	G	741	K	3819

EMBROIDERY AS AN ART FORM

One of the most curious things about embroidery and cross stitch is that it's generally not considered as being an art form. It's a strange phenomenon, but when people think of art, they tend to think of paintings, sculptures or strange conceptual art photography stuff. Rarely do people think of stitcheries.

In her thought-provoking book *The Subversive Stitch* Rozsika Parker explores the tensions between embroidery and art, as well as embroidery and femininity, and it's interesting to consider how linked these two ideas are.

Long story short, men have spent hundreds of years promoting the idea that they're superior to women and, as part of this campaign, the world of art was brought into the argument. While the women sat at home meekly doing embroidery, as a hobby or as a way of maintaining the homestead, the men went off to conquer the world or make big pieces of painted or sculptured art to prove how amazing (!) they were. Because the act of making embroidery is quite restrained, sitting at a hoop and stitching, the very image of a stitcher supported the argument that women were mild mannered and lesser to magnificent men. As I said, it's part of a patriarchal paradigm that's been going for centuries, and this is a book about cross stitch, not gender politics, so I'm not going to launch into a debate on the subject; however, it's interesting to realise how these simple stitches have a connection to such world-shaping views.

A side effect of this debate is that embroidery became disconnected from the mainstream art world and categorised as a pastime or hobby. This is a school of thought that remains to this day, and when you see textile art breaking into the mainstream, it's usually because an already-famous artist has chosen to do work with threads and fabrics – think of Tracey Emin's quilts or Grayson Perry's tapestries. It's rare to find an internationally recognised artist who solely works in thread, or who has risen from the world of embroidery. But believe me, there are thousands of fantastic artists out there whose work will blow you away, yet their chosen medium acts as a barrier to full recognition in the wider artistic context, and our Outlier in this chapter is a perfect example.

I have a fairly blunt view on the world of art, and am convinced that, in the main, it is an exercise in hype. I struggle to grasp that beautiful hand embroideries are considered a craft at best, while other people can paint circles on a wall and be paid thousands of pounds. It's a bit of a con trick and is somewhat based on the aloof nature of art – that it is beyond the grasp of mere mortals. Embroidery is simple to learn and anyone can develop their expressive side using a needle and thread, which democratises art and threatens the perception of value that underpins the whole industry. I see it like this:

✗ If you buy a cross stitch kit and complete it, you have a nice pastime.
✗ If you buy a cross stitch kit, pay attention to the production of it and take time to make it as good as you can, then you're a crafter.
✗ If you buy a kit and modify it in any way to reflect your own views, you're an artist.

It's as simple as that. The expression of self is what makes art and it doesn't matter if you do it with a needle and thread, or a piece of marble and a hammer, or some car parts and a welding torch. Anyone who suggests that the medium of embroidery isn't an art form is missing the point and perpetuating a value-driven industry that prevents most of us from making a living through art. Don't hate that person – they've just not thought about it much.

If you're still reading this discussion, I thank you for letting me rant for a while, and I applaud you as chances are you're considering your position as a stitcher and an artist. Don't let 'old-school' thinking stop you from expressing yourself, and believe in the work you make. If you work at it and you produce art that touches people's souls, you will be rewarded for it. It's not easy, but it could be worse – you could be trying to make art out of ironmongery. Try lugging that around in your bag!

One final thought: people say embroidery isn't art. I say "hold your horses there, sunshine, I've got a little lady who might change your mind!"

MONA

You start with cross stitch and you end up with one of the world's most recognisable pieces of art.

Distilled down into a pixelated design with only 10 colours, this classic portrait is a great optical illusion as well as a familiar face to adorn your walls. And yes, those stitches do follow you around the room!

Design details
Difficulty: easy
Fabric count: 14
Width: 10cm (4in)
Height: 15.75cm (6¼in)
Colours: 10
Stitches: 2,480

Hashtags:
#art
#davinci
#portrait

COLOUR KEY:

A	422
B	522
C	524
D	612
E	676
G	727
H	3046
I	3047
K	3790
M	3799

OUTLIER: SEVERIJA INČIRAUSKAITĖ-KRIAUNEVIČIENĖ

1 When did you first start stitching and how did you find it?

I was never an embroiderer before I started stitching metal. I have tried different techniques and materials – the ones I needed to convey the idea of the work. Cross stitching came along with metal objects; it was part of the concept of the work. Since the first works were about the manifestations of kitsch and tastelessness in daily life, cross stitch seemed like an appropriate means of conveying it. This technique is often associated with banal handicraft of women, and therefore seemed most appropriate to convey banality in daily life. Choosing the most banal flower patterns was based on the same reasons. I did not create these patterns myself on purpose and applied the available unified schemes from women's hobby magazines. As an artist I used the ready-made method, that is, using existing objects to create a piece of art. Old items and cross stitch patterns from magazines are the main artistic material, which helps me tell different stories.

More Than a Hobby
If you needed proof that embroidery is an art form, Severija Inčirauskaitė-Kriaunevičienė has it in spades. And car doors and watering cans and buckets...

2 What was your first transition to metal?

The first work, Life is Beautiful (2005), is a combination of metal and textile. It is a collection of five large pot lids embroidered with flower patterns.

This work was a reference to the Soviet period (my childhood), when the daily life of people was very poor and lacked essential household items. Many people used tasteless and poorly designed things, which were identical to each other across the whole Soviet Union. The understanding of design was very primitive and in bad taste. For example, every kitchen had identical enamel pots decorated with flowers, mushrooms, etc. On the one hand, my reminiscences of that time are very negative; on the other hand, it was the time of my childhood, which had warm memories as well. Therefore, the work speaks of contrasting emotions relating to childhood.

Although the cross stitch patterns are often similar visually, each work has its own idea and tells a different story. One of my first works was the Fall Collection (Rudens Kolekcija), comprising rusty farm tools, created in 2005, when Lithuania had just joined the European Union. At that time, the issue of identity was very relevant in my country ("Won't this membership destroy our uniqueness?"). The corroded tools of Lithuanian farms (watering cans, buckets, milk cans, graters, etc.) addressed the issues of Lithuanian identity related to agrarian culture. And the rust itself (the collection comprised only rusty items) was an essential element of the work. We have a lot of rain

4 The process of stitching on handheld canvas is meditative and soothing – is there a mindfulness to be found in stitching on metal?

When embroidering a large object, such as a car part or piece of wall, one should not expect the calming and meditative effect of embroidery. It is a real workout, because I have to be on both sides of the embroidered object (sticking the thread in and pulling it out). However, with smaller objects, such as plates or spoons, the process is quite calming. Nonetheless, care is always needed, because I do not follow the patterns exactly: I change the colours and patterns and improvise a lot. When creating realistic works, such as the embroidered potatoes in the work Give Us This Day Our Daily Bread... (Kasdienes duonos duok mums šiandien...), I match the colours of threads as a painter matches paint.

5 How do you think your work is evolving?

I believe that my works are becoming more conceptual. While earlier the technological effect (metal and embroidery) used to be enough, it is no

in Lithuania and the corrosion process takes place in a wet environment and, therefore, the rusty objects served as a reference to the Lithuanian climate.

3 What are the technical challenges of using large pieces of metal as your primary surface? (You must be pretty handy with a drill!)

Using a drill is not as complicated as it may seem. Yes, precision and care are essential, because the holes have to be perforated very accurately. However, due to lack of time I no longer drill the holes myself – it is technical work, not creative. I draw an accurate pattern with dots for my assistant and he does the work. Technologically, the most complex work was my last installation, Kill for Peace, for which soldiers' helmets were embroidered. Before perforation, the metal of the helmets had to be softened because very hard tempered metal is used for making helmets. Therefore, this work involved more complex technological processes, not just drilling.

longer surprising and can no longer be the main intrigue about the work. The current issues are important to me and I want to draw attention to them. I cannot close my eyes and remain silent and therefore I choose an active civil position as an artist. Lately my works have more often been presented in modern art galleries and museums, not only in the context of textile art, and bought by significant museums around the world.

PATTERN DESIGN

COMPUTER DESIGN

There are times in your life when you'll want to stop following others and set out on your own. Cross stitch is no different, so let's look at how to make your own patterns.

TECHNOLOGY

If you really want to level up with your cross stitch, then getting a computer program is the key to unlocking your inner designer. There are several products available on the market for PC, Mac and mobile, and I'd encourage you to try them out and see which one works best for you.

I've been using PCStitch for years and find it a great tool to work with. As with most cross stitch software, you can import images and convert them to designs, or build patterns up block by block. The clever bit comes when the software colour matches your image to specific thread colour palettes, so you can choose your favourite brand and work with all their available colours. Good cross stitch software should allow you to do the following:

- ✗ Specify the dimensions of your stitching area, with an adjustment for different counts of fabric (stitches per inch).
- ✗ Enable you to use cross stitch, quarter and three-quarter stitch, backstitch and running stitch.
- ✗ Provide colour palettes for the common thread companies and allow you to set the maximum number of colours in your design.
- ✗ Choose the font or symbols that are used to specify the different colours.
- ✗ Print the design using symbols, colour blocks and a combination of the two.
- ✗ Import images and set parameters to create a colour-matched design.
- ✗ Modify imported images with colour fill, cut and paste and other editing tools.
- ✗ Create designs from scratch and add fonts to your pattern.

And that's just for starters!

While I could get bogged down in the minutiae of how each cross stitch software works, life is short, so I'm going to focus on some of the key principles in working with imported images. In this section we'll explore what happens when you fiddle with the main variables of a cross stitch design:

- ✗ Size
- ✗ Count
- ✗ Colours

And you'll also get a good dose of cross-stitched Vitamin C and manganese!

INTRODUCING THE PINEAPPLE!

Let's start with our first pineapple. Based on a royalty-free image from the internet, this image has been processed through the software, but without any tinkering. The only concession when processing it was that I removed the white background, so it wouldn't influence the colour choice, and I didn't crop the image. So the width of the design is based on the entire image, not just the pineapple itself. The only other limitations I placed on the design in most cases were having no more than 16 colours in the palette and I deliberately chose to ignore backstitching. We clear?

First off, straight off the bat, it's our friend the 6-inch pineapple on 14-count fabric! He's a handsome chap and does look like a pineapple. The design space is 15.25cm (6in) wide, and with 16 colours the pattern weighs in at 3,124 stitches, so it would take a good few hours to complete. The balance between light and shade is not bad, although a bit of tinkering with colour saturation would improve things. However, as a basic design it's fairly solid, so you can feel free to stitch it yourself if you'd like!

Design details
Difficulty: medium
Fabric count: 14
Width: 15.25cm (6in)
Height: 21.3cm (8⅜in)
Colours: 16
Stitches: 3,124

Hashtags:
#food
#portrait
#realism

COLOUR KEY:

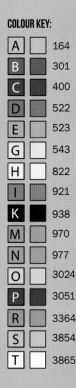

A		164
B		301
C		400
D		522
E		523
G		543
H		822
I		921
K		938
M		970
N		977
O		3024
P		3051
R		3364
S		3854
T		3865

Size

The size of your fabric is the first major parameter to deal with, as it forms the basis of your design. Simply put, the bigger your piece of fabric, the better your ability to add detail to your stitching. There are trade-offs between the size of the design and the length of time you want to spend stitching it, and that choice is for you and you alone.

This table throws a bunch of numbers at you to explain the variety of stitch counts that can be achieved by varying the size of your fabric, and for ease I'm working on 14-count Aida, so 14 stitches per inch!

Fabric width	Number of rows	Number of columns	Total potential stitches
1-inch	14	14	196
2-inch	28	28	784
4-inch	56	56	3,136
6-inch	84	84	7,056
10-inch	140	140	19,600
12-inch	168	168	28,224

As you can see, the numbers scale up pretty quickly so if you're looking for something detailed, you might want to scale it up, or you might need to vary the density of the fabric.

Let's take our pineapple friend and spin him through a few sizes to see how the image changes as we increase the size.

Pineapple: 1-inch 14-count

At the smallest setting the pineapple is extremely blocky, but looks like a pineapple if you squint at it. Even at this micro level the software has extracted 14 colours from the image, although some of them will only be for a few stitches. It's the kind of pineapple you can bang out in a hurry – an emergency pineapple, if you will.

Design details
Difficulty: easy
Fabric count: 14
Width: 2.5cm (1in)
Height: 3.8cm (1½in)
Colours: 14
Stitches: 121

EPIC PINEAPPLE

We've explored the three variables of size, fabric count and colour and seen the different effects you can get by changing them. There's a lot of flexibility in achieving the outcome you want while still keeping the design within realistic size constraints, and therefore within a reasonable time scale to complete. Cross stitching takes time and there's only so fast that anyone can stitch, despite all the gizmos you can get, so if you're planning a design and there's a deadline involved, then you'll want to keep it simple where you can.

Of course, sometimes a simple design isn't going to cut it. Sometimes a small cross stitch isn't going to have enough impact. Sometimes you just need to go large, so here it is – the Epic Pineapple.

This is the biggest pattern in this whole book: 12 inches wide on 14-count fabric; it's not going to be completed overnight, but if you want a super-realistic looking pineapple, here you are!

With nearly 12,000 stitches, this is a serious design (and for that reason I haven't included a chart for it!), but it really looks like a detailed pineapple, even with just 16 colours. The number of stitches means that the colours balance out better as they are more focused.

We've established that it's possible to translate anything into cross stitch and identified that there are compromises that you might need to make. If you want to finish a piece quickly, then you might want something smaller, but this means an image that is more pixelated and graphic than the original. Alternatively, if you're prepared to have a large-scale, or high-density image, you can create some fantastic effects, as long as you have the time.

Here's a tip for you. Spend an hour cross stitching squares of 10 by 10 stitches. Just use one colour and see how many you can stitch. Once you know what your pace is under these test conditions, you can halve it and get a fair sense of how long it might take you to stitch a multicoloured pattern in normal circumstances.

The realistic effect isn't for everyone, and there's a lot of skill involved in paring back an image to a simpler, more graphic design; however, if you want to make portraits or accurate creations, we've identified what it'll take!

Design details
Difficulty: hard
Fabric count: 14
Width: 30.5cm (12in)
Height: 42.5cm (16¾in)
Colours: 16
Stitches: 11,725

Hashtags:
#food
#portrait
#realism

PORTRAIT OF A PINEAPPLE

Thus far we've looked at the whole of the pineapple and seen how realistic we can make things if we wish. But what's great about cross stitch software is how you can crop and edit images to suit your needs. So instead of a whole pineapple, we can focus in on one aspect of this fine fruit to truly appreciate the beauty in its creation.

Design details
Difficulty: hard
Fabric count: 14
Width: 15.25cm (6in)
Height: 31.1cm (12¼in)
Colours: 16
Stitches: 9,486

Hashtags:
#food
#portrait
#realism

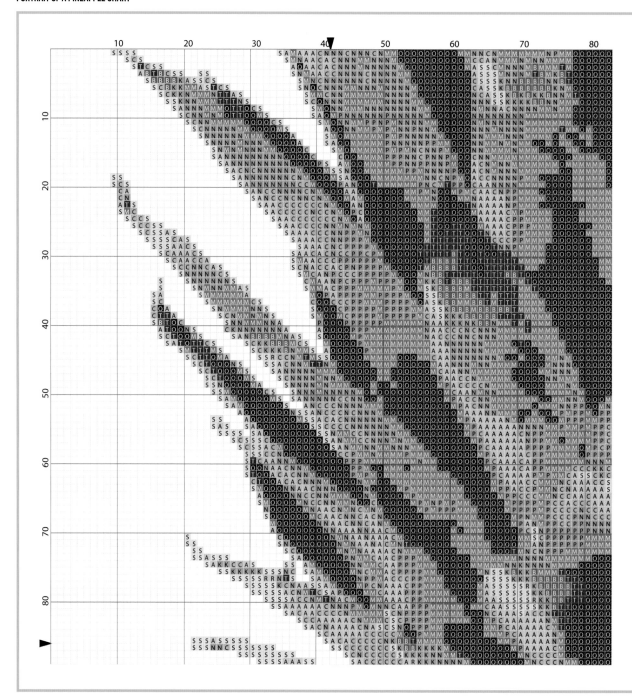

COLOUR KEY:

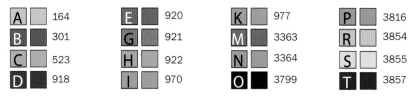

A	164	E	920	K	977	P	3816
B	301	G	921	M	3363	R	3854
C	523	H	922	N	3364	S	3855
D	918	I	970	O	3799	T	3857

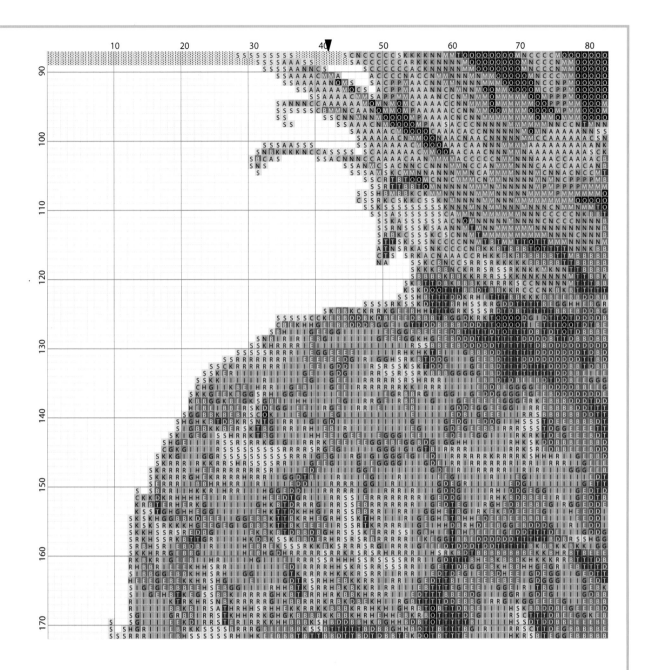

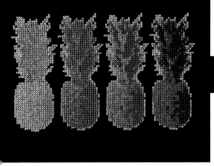

POP ART PINEAPPLE

Once you've wrapped your head around how to get the size and density of design that you like, don't feel restricted to just keep things familiar. Why not bust out the colours and try something a bit different?

Enter the Pop Art Pineapple! This design is based on a 3-inch version of our beloved pineapple, on 14-count fabric. Once I'd got the basic design, I duplicated it three more times and then started playing with the colours. Fortunately, it was not too difficult to pull together a colour palette for each design, and then to replace specific colours with the new ones, and – hey presto – pop art!

This is where cross stitch designing can get exciting. It's one thing to take an image and turn it into cross stitch, but it's so much more fun to start playing with the images, and remixing them to make new ideas. Any decent software should allow you to copy, paste and flip parts of the design, as well as overlaying text and manipulating colours, so the sky really is the limit as to what can be done. It's at this point where cross stitch software comes into its own, as it offers editing possibilities that would be hard to achieve on paper.

While you can easily create patterns from scratch, it's a lot easier to import raw materials into the software and play with them to see what happens. I'll often import an image into software to see what colours get picked, and then use that palette as a starting point for a new design.

Don't be afraid to emulate the work of artists that you admire to see if you can translate them into cross stitch, or to seek out images from the internet that suit your tastes. (A point of note: imitation is the sincerest form of flattery, but stealing other people's work is never cool, so tread that line very carefully!)

The more you use your software, the more you'll unlock ideas about what can be done, and your design sensibilities will evolve. Even through the process of making this book I've pushed at certain boundaries, particularly towards three-quarter stitches and stretched myself, and I feel better for doing so.

What's great about the software is that it's easy to try new things and no one gets hurt in the process, so you can make design after design until you're at a point that you are comfortable with.

I don't really have that much design wisdom, but one thing I do know is that you have to keep making things, and at some point you'll make something half decent. You can't expect to produce well-designed patterns straight away, but if you persevere, you'll discover your creative voice and be able to express it more clearly. So get stuck in, and remember what Picasso said: "Inspiration exists, but it has to find you working".

Design details
Difficulty: hard
Fabric count: 14
Width: 16.5cm (6½in)
Height: 10cm (4in)
Colours: 29
Stitches: 3,388

Hashtags:
#food
#lifeiscolorful
#popart
#realism

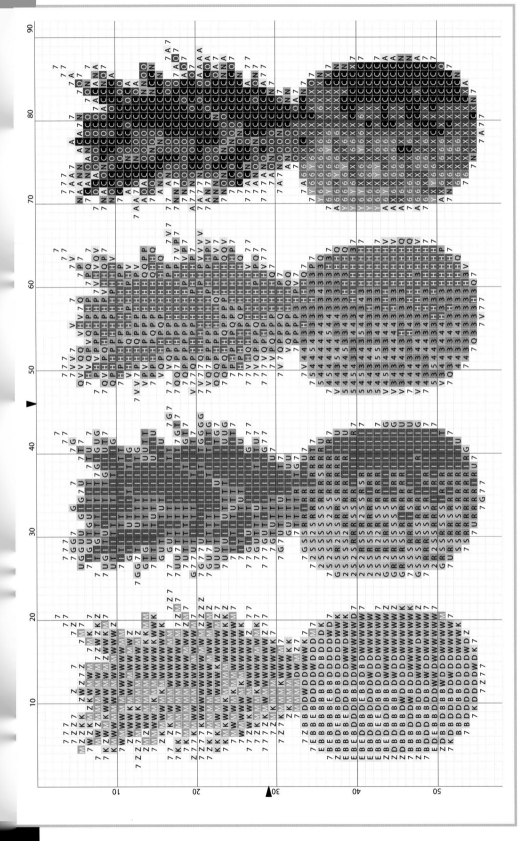

COLOUR KEY:

A		162
B		307
C		336
D		444
E		445
G		564
H		666
I		701
K		726
M		783
N		813
O		825
P		893
Q		894
R		906
S		907
T		912
U		954
V		963
W		972
X		995
Y		996
Z		3078
2		3348
3		3705
4		3706
5		3708
6		3843
7		3865

Kickin' it old school

Let's not forget that you can still plan out cross stitch designs using graph paper and pencil as well. For artists who work with their hands, rather than directly onto computer, this is a good way to get the initial plans out of your head and into a grid format. The flexibility that comes from using computer software is useful when editing and refining the design, but there's nothing wrong with going analogue and using paper and pen.

All it takes is some graph paper, a pencil, an eraser and some coloured pens to get going. By translating a design into pixels on paper, you're bound to gain a greater appreciation of the form, and the inherent restrictions that can occur when converting curves into squares. This may inform your design process and steer you in different directions than if you rely on software to do all the grunt work for you.

Why not try drawing a familiar object on some graph paper to see how it works as a pixelated image? Most images can be broken down into basic shapes, and if those shapes are square, then you're in luck! Designing on paper might mean you have to be a bit more creative with your colour choices and actually pick them by using your eyes, but if it doesn't kill you, it'll make you stronger, so don't be afraid to give it a go!

Having said all that, you'd expect that the next pattern was one that I'd designed on paper, so let's just pretend that happened and that I'm something like a phenomenon. After all, it's only the most complicated pattern in the whole book, so why would I rely on computer software for that?!

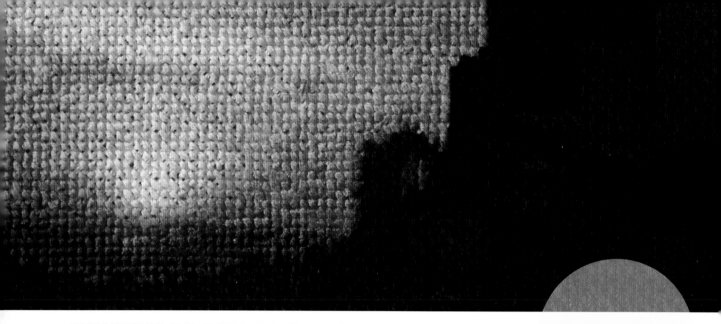

WHITBY ABBEY AT SUNSET

Back in 2011, I took part in a needlework competition at the Yorkshire Fair in the UK that was filmed as part of the Kirstie Allsopp TV series, *Kirstie's Handmade Britain*. The theme of the competition was Yorkshire and I created *Whitby Abbey at Sunset*, a huge design with 99 colours. Yes, that's right, 99 colours! I made the design decision to stitch it on black canvas, which meant that I didn't stitch the Abbey, just the fantastic sunset behind it – but I allowed the software to choose as many colours as it wanted to get the most photorealistic sunset possible.

Jump to the day of the competition and I was pitted against members of the Yorkshire Women's Institute, some fellow competitors and the mighty Kirstie Allsopp, whom I ♥ a great deal indeed.

The competition was judged fairly with all entries being anonymous and Kirstie took the win with a mixed media cushion. My design, despite being very impressive looking, didn't fare so well. However, because Kirstie got help with hers and had won some of the other competitions in her TV series, by the time the show aired most people thought that I'd been robbed and should have won!

It was quite the experience and I learned some valuable lessons:

✗ Stitching to a deadline can really hamper your enjoyment of cross stitch. I spent the whole weekend before the show cross stitching for 18 hours a day and went a bit loopy.
✗ When stitching for competitions, it's the quality of the stitching that is paramount. Better to stitch 800 railroaded stitches that sit perfectly, than 8,000 stitches that are a bit rushed and twisted.
✗ You can't sticky tape a cross stitch into a frame and expect to get away with it.
✗ Failure on national TV can often work to your advantage.
✗ 99 colours are a lot to deal with and this comes at quite a cost, but it does create a spectacular effect.

So here you have it, *Whitby Abbey at Sunset* – proof that if you allow your software total freedom to colour-match threads, it can produce amazing things. Admittedly, some of the colours have only two or three stitches, but hey, look at it. It's gorgeous!

Design details
Difficulty: hard
Fabric count: 18
Width: 21cm (8¼in)
Height: 11.5cm (4½in)
Colours: 99
Stitches: 8,296

Hashtags:
#landscape
#lifeiscolorful
#realism

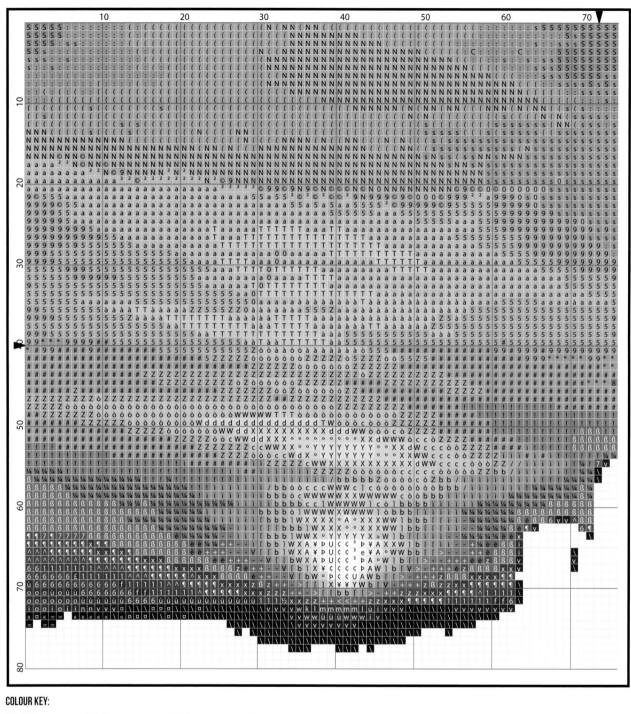

COLOUR KEY:

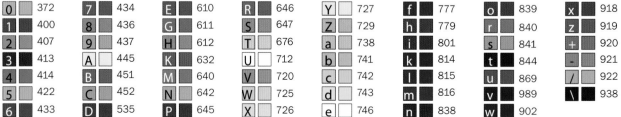

0	372	7	434	E	610	R	646	Y	727	f	777	o	839	x	918
1	400	8	436	G	611	S	647	Z	729	h	779	r	840	z	919
2	407	9	437	H	612	U	712	a	738	i	801	s	841	+	920
3	413	A	445	K	632	V	720	b	741	k	814	t	844	-	921
4	414	B	451	M	640	W	725	c	742	l	815	u	869	/	922
5	422	C	452	N	642	X	726	d	743	m	816	v	989	\	938
6	433	D	535	P	645			e	746	n	838	w	902		

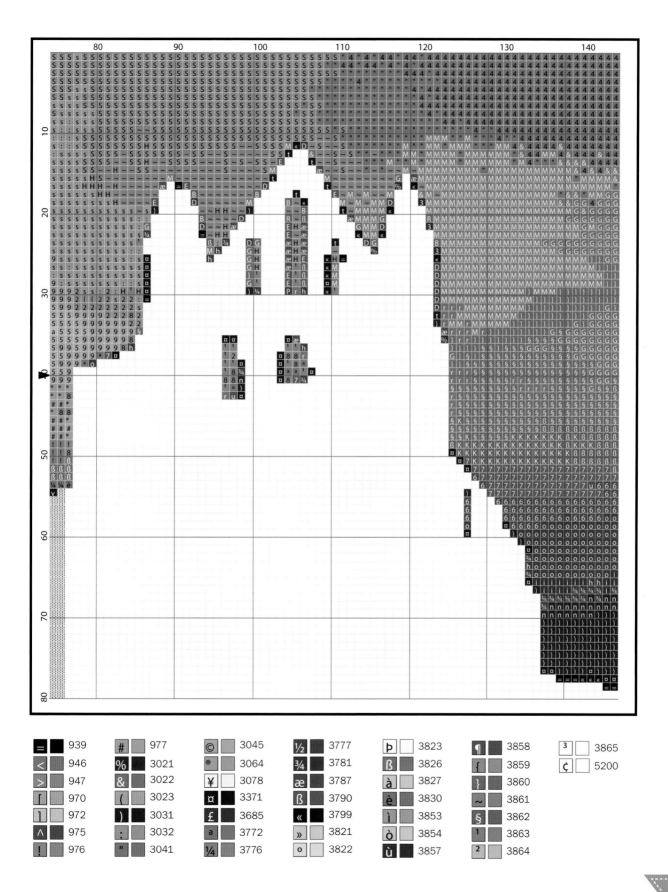

= 939	# 977	© 3045	½ 3777	þ 3823	¶ 3858	3 3865
< 946	% 3021	◎ 3064	¾ 3781	ß 3826	ſ 3859	ç 5200
> 947	& 3022	¥ 3078	æ 3787	à 3827	} 3860	
Γ 970	(3023	¤ 3371	ß 3790	è 3830	~ 3861	
] 972	) 3031	£ 3685	« 3799	ì 3853	§ 3862	
∧ 975	: 3032	a 3772	» 3821	ò 3854	1 3863	
! 976	" 3041	¼ 3776	o 3822	ù 3857	2 3864	

OUTLIER: LORD LIBIDAN

Pattern Design
Lord Libidan's video game- and pop culture-inspired designs are the quintessence of computer-based cross stitch creativity.

1 When did you first start stitching and how did you find it?

The summer of 2009. I started stitching a few years before it started to really take off in Britain, and I fell into it by mistake. I bought something in a department store and I got a free 1-inch Highland cow kit. As always with English summers, it rained for weeks on end and so I found myself twiddling my thumbs. I gave the cow a shot and finished it that afternoon. I went to the store the next day to get another one and I was hooked. I've had at least one project on the go ever since.

It took only three projects before I started having my own ideas on what might make an interesting topic, so I dropped the kits for my own patterns. However, that Highland cow still sits on my desk today as a reminder.

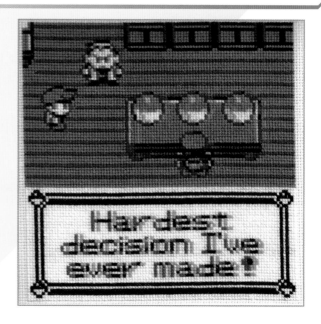

2 You design using software; tell me a bit about that.

Paper allows you to get a quick idea down, or a small stitch; however, as soon as it gets a little bigger, you never have enough paper, or you have to move things around, or you don't have enough coloured pens handy.

Design software allows you to quickly and easily throw a pattern together with masses of possibilities. If I want to recreate the Mona Lisa, the first place I start is with an image of the real artwork. I import it into the program, set the size I want to stitch and the number of colours and I get an instant result.

Sure, it may not work the first time; in fact, it almost never does. But now you can edit the image further, change the thread count, size, colours. And then you can go even further down, moving individual stitches, or whole parts to make a better pattern. You can then view it in representative stitches and see what it would look like with different Aida, or add in special stitches to finish it off perfectly.

Software allows all that to happen within minutes. I tend to spend hours pulling something together to be perfect in my eyes – however, you're saving so much time on a paper pattern.

There are many processes out there to make patterns, each varying slightly with the programs you use, but the general process is the same. Once you have a rough idea of the size of the piece, you start making the main

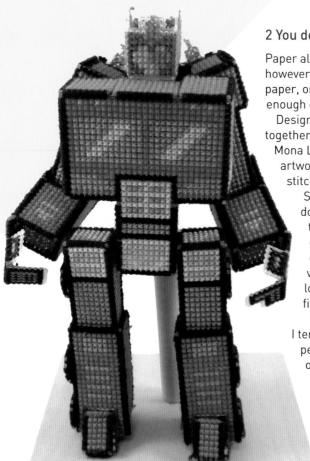

part first; a main character or a point of interest. You then build out the parts around it bit by bit (normally in unrealistic colours). Once you have a rough idea you fix the colours, and then add the smaller details; adding variance to a plain wall, or detailing the hero's pose better. Once you're done you can export into an image or a pdf pattern like the ones you get in kits.

However, that said, I still use paper sometimes. When making a 3D piece I cut out squared paper to represent the canvas, and tape it together. The tactile feedback you get from paper for a 3D project (see the Transformers, below and opposite, below) helps massively.

3 You're not afraid to think outside the hoop with your designs – what inspires you to push at these boundaries?

Originally, it started with me simply not knowing the boundaries. When I first picked up cross stitch I had no preconceived ideas of what was possible, or what other people were doing; I stitched from a point of complete ignorance.

After I had finished a few pieces, I gleaned an understanding of what I could do and what I couldn't. However, I've never been one to give something up and it was only when I was stuck that I started looking at the work of others. It not only opened up the world of cross stitch out there to me, but the simplest of things that someone else may have done could solve the issue I was having.

It's this feeling of a slight ambivalence at my own skill level that I try to hold on to. I never categorise myself in a skill boundary. I'm not an advanced stitcher, or even a beginner; to me, I'm a complete neophyte, a novice always willing to learn.

With the knowledge that I can fail, I'm free to take a punt on something. I pick up a needle and don't think about how possible it is to stitch the inside of a right-angled corner; instead, I just try. When I fail I try it a different way. The only way to push a boundary is to forget the boundary is there at all.

4 The process of cross stitch can be meditative and soothing – what are your thoughts on this?

Cross stitch requires dexterity, forward planning and accuracy, all of which demand attention. However, these are all skills you practise every day, and so you can stitch with your mind on something else at the same time. A lot of people liken it to knitting in this aspect, allowing you to chat at the same time, but cross stitch goes a little further and bolsters that by allowing you to make mistakes.

In fact, when I come across an issue, I don't get mad or confused; I just start unpicking. Fixing a mistake is almost part of the process. Nothing ever goes your way all the time, and cross stitch is the same; however, you're stitching on your terms. It allows you to take it easy, relax into the stitching. Yes, you could go hell for leather and stitch something as fast as possible, but I'd much prefer to stitch while watching TV and drinking tea. The great thing about the meditative effect of cross stitch is that it's a positive feedback. Normal meditation ends when it ends. But completing a row of stitches, or a pattern, even the completed project – you get a sense of accomplishment. And there's always time for just one more stitch...

THINKING OUTSIDE THE HOOP

IF IT'S GOT HOLES IN IT...

...then you should consider it as a potential surface for stitching!

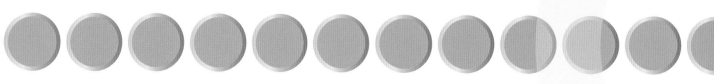

Cross stitch tends to be confined to fabric and then framed or stuck in a hoop. On a good day it makes it to a chair covering or an embellishment on some clothing, but rarely do these beloved stitches get to break free and run amok in the world.

The good news is that things are changing and there are a number of platforms on which you can stitch, and in this section we'll explore some of these ideas. Cross stitch relies on a structured grid to maintain its composure, and if you're looking to stitch on new surfaces, you'll need to replicate that grid to achieve that proper cross stitch effect.

Recent developments by the thread companies provide clever ways to stitch on other fabric surfaces, using soluble plastic interface and pull-away paper interface. Either of these provide a template that can be placed over a different surface to create the grid and, most importantly, they can be removed after you've finished.

You can use those products as templates for working with different surfaces as well, and there's no harm in getting a piece of wood and a tiny drill to emblazon a chair with a new design, for example, drilling holes through the grid where you need them.

If you want inspiration in that direction, look back at the mixed media work of Severija Inčirauskaitė-Kriaunevičienė (see pages 90–91). All it takes is a drill, a grid template and some courage, and before you know it you'll be stitching on everything!

For now, let's keep things simple and look at a few examples of different surfaces you can stitch on that already have holes in them.

Design details
Difficulty: easy
Fabric count: 14
Width: 7.9cm (3⅛in)
Height: 2.8cm (1⅛in)
Colours: 5
Stitches: 411

BLING

Everybody deserves a bit of bling in their lives and you don't get more bling than a piece of personalised jewellery. You can find leather wristbands with a grid of holes on them from a few different retailers – use your favourite search engine to find them.

In this instance, I've taken a brown strap and gone for five shades of gold to create a 3D embossed effect that's just a little bit gangster. Watch out for those three-quarter stitches – you'll need to pierce the leather with your needle to make them work (see chart on page 122).

Hashtags:
#backstitch
#leather
#threequarterstitch
#typography

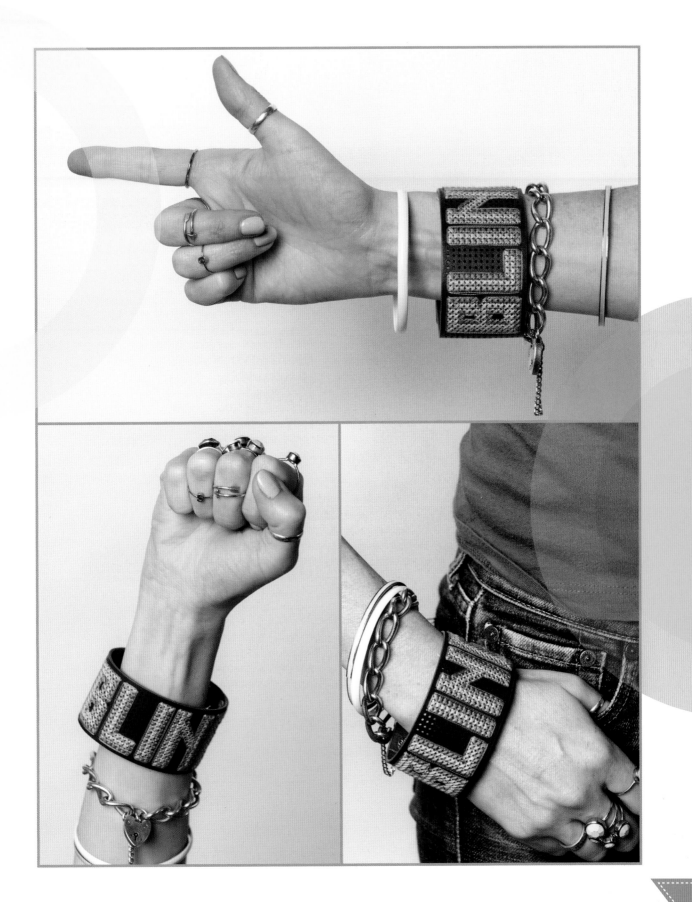

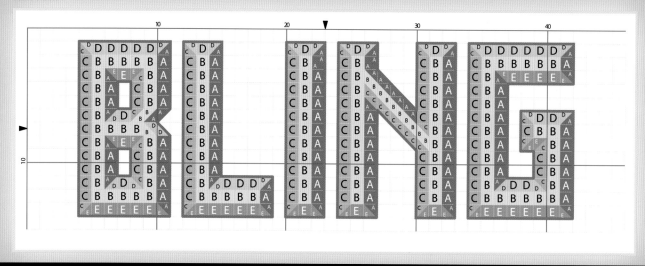

COLOUR KEY:

A	3829	C	729	E	680	
B	3855	D	676			

Backstitch lines:
——————— 3829

STITCHING ON PLASTIC

Plastic canvas has been around for a while and is a great surface to cross stitch on. Whether it's 5-count canvas that is ideal for younger stitchers, or the more familiar 14-count, it's definitely something you should try out.

You may recall how our Pattern Design Outlier, Lord Libidan, made Transformers using plastic canvas – they actually change shape – and once you start playing with the idea of three dimensions and wrap your head around the best methods of construction, a whole new world opens up for you.

Plastic canvas is robust and great for using in unusual environments, whether it's sticking some cross stitched graffiti on a wall somewhere, or merely stitching something to go in your shed. (I'm planning to stitch a Watch Your Head sign for my shed, but I've banged my bonce so many times, I keep forgetting...)

Plastic canvas is firmer than fabric and, while this is helpful in the main part, when it comes to finishing off and wheedling that needle under existing stitches, it can prove a bit tricky. Consider using an embroidery needle, as the pointed end is better at getting under the stitches than its rounder tapestry cousin.

Lastly, the best thing about plastic canvas is that it's firm and it means that you don't need to frame your work, you can just cut it out and stick it wherever. You can design pieces of any shape, trim around the canvas and create mini masterpieces that can go anywhere, from your desk to your car to a galaxy far, far away...

Stitch Invaders

Presenting a trio of super spaceships for stitching on plastic canvas. Stitch them, trim round them (leaving at least one square's width around the edge of the design) and then you can take them to infinity and beyond!

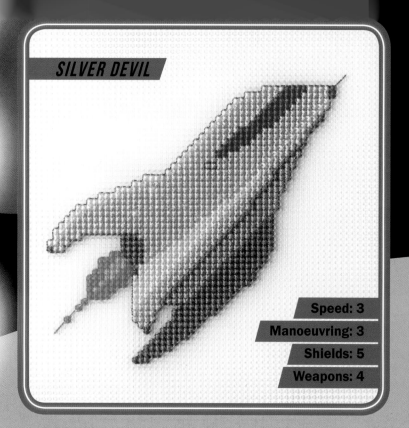

SILVER DEVIL

Speed:	3
Manoeuvring:	3
Shields:	5
Weapons:	4

Design details
Difficulty: easy
Fabric count: 14
Width: 10cm (4in)
Height: 10cm (4in)
Colours: 7
Stitches: 1,023

Hashtags:
#backstitch
#geekcraft
#plastic
#scifi

SILVER DEVIL CHART

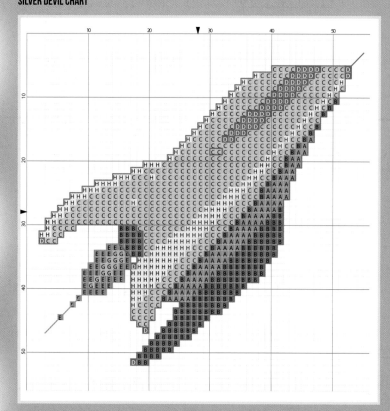

A		318
B		414
C		415
D		600
E		608
G		741
H		762

Backstitch lines:
——— 414
——— 600
········· 608

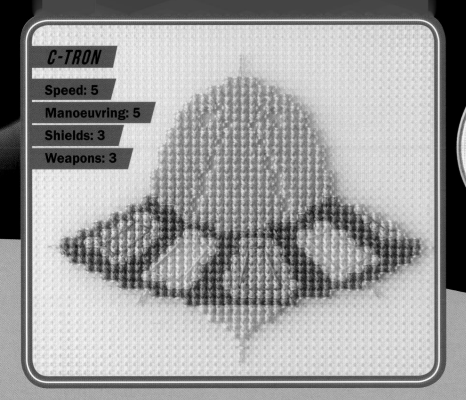

C-TRON

Speed: 5

Manoeuvring: 5

Shields: 3

Weapons: 3

Design details
Difficulty: easy
Fabric count: 14
Width: 7.3cm (2⅞in)
Height: 9.5cm (3¾in)
Colours: 5
Stitches: 661

C-TRON CHART

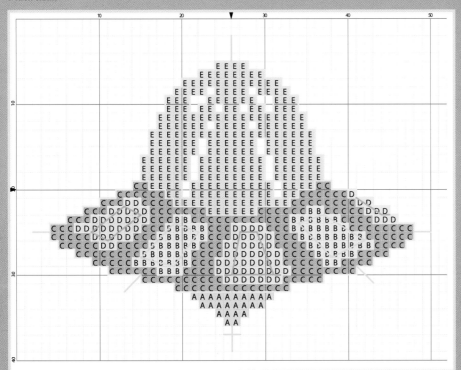

		307
A		307
B		445
C		704
D		772
E		955

Backstitch lines:

——— 307   ——— 704
——— 445   ——— 772

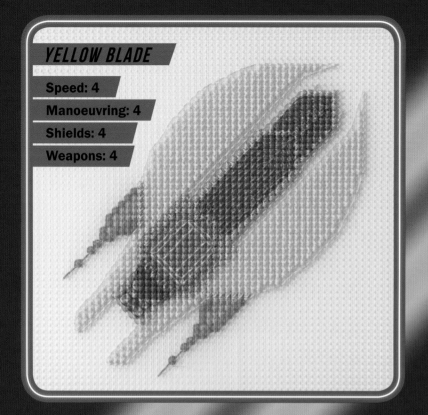

YELLOW BLADE

Speed: 4

Manoeuvring: 4

Shields: 4

Weapons: 4

Design details
Difficulty: easy
Fabric count: 14
Width: 10cm (3½in)
Height: 10cm (3½in)
Colours: 7
Stitches: 1,067

YELLOW BLADE CHART

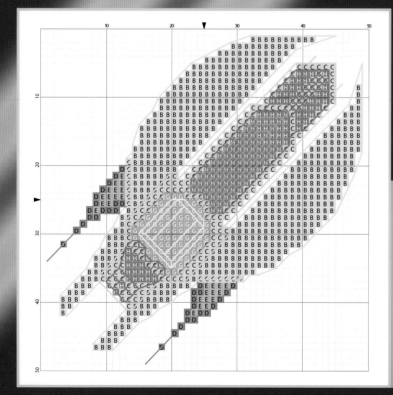

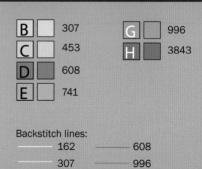

Hashtags:
#backstitch
#geekcraft
#plastic
#scifi

B		307
C		453
D		608
E		741

| G | | 996 |
| H | | 3843 |

Backstitch lines:
—— 162   —— 608
—— 307   —— 996
—— 453   —— 3843

STITCHING ON METAL

Arguably the most hardcore stitching happens on metal and I'll just come out and say that it's a lot easier to stitch on metal with pre-existing holes than it is to create your own. If you are going to break out and stitch on a metal surface without holes, please take care and do not forget those safety glasses!

There are plenty of metal surfaces that have holes you can try stitching on. A great place to start is with a sieve; it comes with a grid formation and a useful handle to hold and to hang it up with. My chums at the Royal School of Needlework (shameless name drop) use sieves in their degree courses to move away from flat planes and to play with perspective and curves.

Thin metals such as aluminium foil are easy to pierce with a needle and make more of an interesting backdrop for your art. You can use a grid from plastic canvas or some of the other interfaces we've mentioned, so that your stitching is aligned correctly. Or you can just throw caution to the wind and stitch it however you like – just remember to call it a punk aesthetic and you'll get away with it!

One of the best recent discoveries in this territory is the Algot shelf range from the home furnishing phenomenon that is Ikea. It's a white metal shelf with a grid of holes on it and it's ideal for a bit of stitched wall art. There's a caveat here, as the spacing of the holes is quite wide and makes it difficult to do cross stitches that look like blocks of colour, rather than Xs, so I thought I'd bust out the backstitch for a spot of optical awesomeness – LOOK!

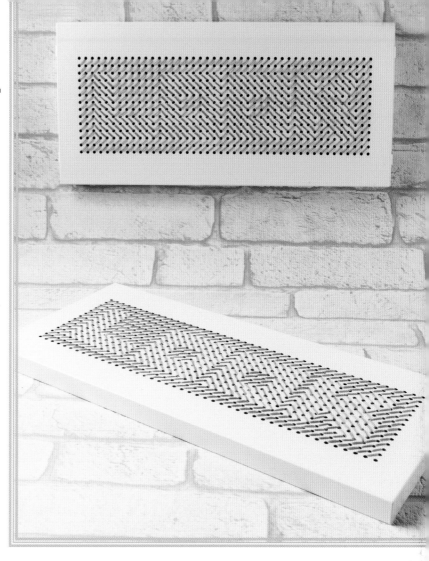

LOOK!

Guaranteed to make your eyes boggle, but also guaranteed to get people paying attention, this nifty backstitched typographic illusion is a great thing to stick on your wall. The Algot shelf is white and will therefore fit in any room – why not stitch this in an accent colour from your favourite room?

Design details
Difficulty: easy
Fabric count: 3
Width: 36.8cm (14½in)
Height: 13.5cm (5¼in)
Colours: 1
Stitches: 217
(backstitch)

Hashtags:
#metal
#typography

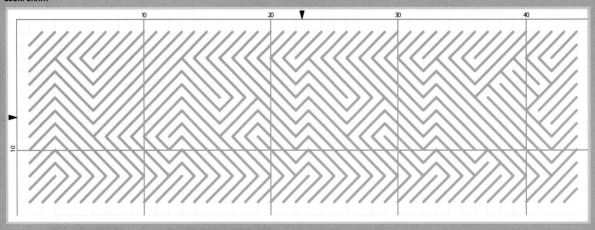

Backstitch lines:
—————— 996

What The?!

One of the most under-appreciated cross stitch formats is the handy coaster. Whether it's the protection of your wooden furniture, or the demarcation of your office space, a bespoke cross stitched coaster can come in useful. They're also pretty simple gifts for people, particularly if you personalise the content to suit the recipient. There's a fair range of sizes and shapes, and they're simple enough to work with, so why not have a go?

In this instance, I've decided to immortalise the kind of response that normally comes from knocking that mid-morning cup of coffee all over your desk, or in your lap. We've all been there and it's always the day you decide to wear something light – son of a biscuit!

Design details
Difficulty: easy
Fabric count: 14
Width: 10cm (4in)
Height: 10cm (4in)
Colours: 3
Stitches: 2,746

Hashtags:
#nsfw
#plastic
#popart
#typography

COLOUR KEY:

A	⬛	310
B	⬜ (grey)	318
C	⬜	762

WE'RE ALL ADULTS…

So let's talk about adult content. Swearing in cross stitch is a thing, as is swearing in real life. There's no point in pretending that it isn't and, for many people, a bit of cross stitch with some fruity language is their first introduction to the craft. There's not a lot of harm in it.

There are plenty of embroideries out there that feature subjects that might make you blush, and even stuff that'll make your eyes water. Believe me, I've seen it. Sure, it's not everyone's taste, but art exists in all forms and whether you like it or not, there is a place for it. I argue that when someone pushes at a boundary, such as that of good taste, it creates a space wherein other people can come and explore.

In 2006, Julie Jackson's *Subversive Cross Stitch* book changed the world of cross stitch and inspired a generation of snarky stitchers, myself included, with the classic combination of flowery borders and fruity phrases. Since then, there have been many people who've combined crass language and cross stitches for the amusement of others.

Gangster cross stitch is also an emerging trend with the hardness of hip-hop blending nicely with the charm of cross stitch, and you'll find people mashing up needlework with death metal, satanic phrases and all manner of darkness. And why not? I'm pretty sure it's hard to remain in a place of fundamental darkness while finishing off some tidy backstitch…

We shouldn't overlook erotic embroidery and nudey needlework, as there are many instances where people have used a needle and thread to explore body issues and sexuality. If you look hard enough (pardon the pun) you can find naughty images stitched into the Bayeux Tapestry, reinforcing the fact that, for as long as there's been art, there's been subversive art.

Needlework is largely considered 'nice' and 'safe' and this school of thought creates a tension when exploring adult content – artists can create more of a stir by stitching something rude, but at the same time people's sensibilities seem to be more precious when being confronted with erotic embroidery. It's a peculiarity that you don't find in the more mainstream art practices.

Political comment is another topic that features in all art forms and equally so in embroidery. As we've seen with the Craftivism topic, needlework provides a good opportunity to express your political views through peaceful process, but many people take the concept further and use needlecraft for social critique.

The impact of this work is often greater than with some other forms of expression – it might take a few hours to create a wall mural with paint, but it will often take weeks to produce a topical tapestry, and there's an implicit understanding of that fact with the audience. People recognise the lengthy production time and it gives the work even more gravitas and arguably more power.

The funny thing is, the process of stitching is so soothing that any actual anger that is the motivation for some naughty needlework is usually gone before the piece is finished, so a sense of humour is usually the best accompaniment for anything in this ballpark. It's up to you if you want to do some sweary stitching, but just remember, it's not mean if it's hilarious.

OUTLIER: LES DEUZ'BRO

Thinking Outside the Hoop
Forget yarnbombing. Les Deuz'Bro have been busting boundaries by taking cross stitch out into the wild for everyone to enjoy.

1 What was your first transition to working with fences?

We were together in a same textile design school in the Paris area. We obtained a BA, Anna with a speciality in embroidery and me (Christofer) in textile weaving. Anna worked on a collection of embroideries based on the city, far from the familiar ideas of home. We exhibited our diploma collections together in a show in Paris in September 2013. I was fascinated by her work and always wanted to do something in the street. Anna was a little afraid of working alone so we decided to work together. A few weeks later, for a trade show, we started working directly in the street, doing embroidery without having requested permission. The embroidery was destroyed a day later.

2 What are the technical challenges of using large pieces of wire fence as your primary surface?

We try to work on the street as much as we can. But depending on the project, we have two different ways of working. The first is working directly on fences in the street where we live, in the Paris area. We create typefaces, monograms, patterns and we take measurements and try to accommodate everything before we start. As it takes a lot of time to stitch, we have to organise everything well in advance. We take everything we need with us and start without talking. We've worked outside at all times of the day and night, and in all weathers; we've stitched in snow, rain, in the cold and the heat. It's pretty hard to find the right time to work, but we absolutely love working outside; we like the conversations we have with people walking by.

The second way of working is at home, especially when we are creating something for a specific place abroad. We stitch the piece at home on some fencing, then one of us takes it with us in a suitcase to attach in situ at its destination.

3 The process of stitching on handheld canvas is meditative and soothing – is there a mindfulness to be found in stitching on metal?

I think there is no difference for us working on canvas or a fence. It's just adapting the cross stitch embroidery technique to a new medium. For me (Christofer), it gives exactly the same feeling of meditation as 'traditional' embroidery or other techniques such as weaving. We usually stitch for around 4 to 8 hours on the street – we talk a lot, but we also have really long periods of just working without saying a word.

4 How do you think your work is evolving?

We constantly try to create bigger embroideries and get involved in projects such as set design and teaching. I think our next step is to have a proper space/workshop to create and think about our projects. We also want to involve different techniques at some point, not just cross stitch.

FINAL THOUGHTS

All good things come to an end, and here we are at the final part of *The Mr X Stitch Guide to Cross Stitch*! Hopefully, you've found this book to be useful, inspirational and mildly amusing. Hopefully, you've learned how to cross stitch, how to design your own patterns and the Outliers have shown what is possible if you really put your mind to it. Hopefully, you've read all the words in this book and have learned something new along the way.

I've put my heart into this book and tried to design patterns that you'll enjoy stitching and that you'll find a use for. I've tried to touch on the main themes of cross stitch, from nature and landscapes to sci-fi and flowers, and thrown in a few new ideas such as 3D effects and optical illusions.

If you're an experienced stitcher, I'm hoping that there's been something of use in here, and I hope that you like it enough to share it with people who ought to fall in love with cross stitch like the rest of us. As we've seen, cross stitch is far more than just a hobby and is good for your soul on so many levels that it's almost imperative that you get your stitch on every once in a while. Whether it's stitching something that glows in the dark, or stitching on a non-fabric surface, I hope you've found something that tickles your fancy and makes your day that bit better.

I'd love to hear what you think of the book and to see pictures of your stitching successes. In the resources list opposite you'll find all the places online you can find me, so don't be afraid to get in touch, particularly if you've nice things to share!

I never thought that cross stitch would change my life but it has, and I hope that I've been able to share my passion for this remarkable craft. It's rare to find something that is so intrinsically woven into the cultures of countries across the world, and that has been around for centuries, yet these humble Xs are ubiquitous and are likely to remain that way for years to come.

I wish you many, many happy stitches, and hope that this book gives you even more enthusiasm to connect with this craft and explore your own artistic path through the power of needle and thread.

Big love,

Jamie 'Mr X Stitch' Chalmers
Bedford, August 2017

Mr X Stitch's Jargon Buster

If you really want to blend in with other needlecraft ninjas, you need to know the slang, so you can parlay with other cross stitchers without looking daft. Fortunately, with the Mr X Stitch Jargon Buster (patent pending), you'll be able to rap with the best of them.

Confetti: Lots of scattered single stitches of colour in a WIP

FFS: One of many phrases that you might utter when realising that you have to do some...

Frogging: The miserable act of unpicking stitches – rip it, rip it, rip it!

MSAL: Mystery StitchAlong – you won't know what it is right away.

ORT: Old Ratty Threads – those cut-off bits of thread that you can't bear to part with.

PILF: Pattern I'm Looking For.

Railroading: Making your threads lie flat next to one another in a stitch, rather than letting them lie twisted.

SAL: StitchAlong – an episodic stitchy project that's normally completed over a few months.

Skein: Approximately 8.7 yards (8 metres) of embroidery floss.

Stash: It's your stash, ain't it?

UFO: Unfinished Object – can often be older than your children.

X Stitch: Like cross stitch, but more badass.

WIP: Work in Progress – can easily become a UFO.

WTF: Something you might say when you discover an unexpected knotty mess on the back of your work.

ALPHABET FONTS

abcde
fghijkl
mnopq
rstuvw
xyz

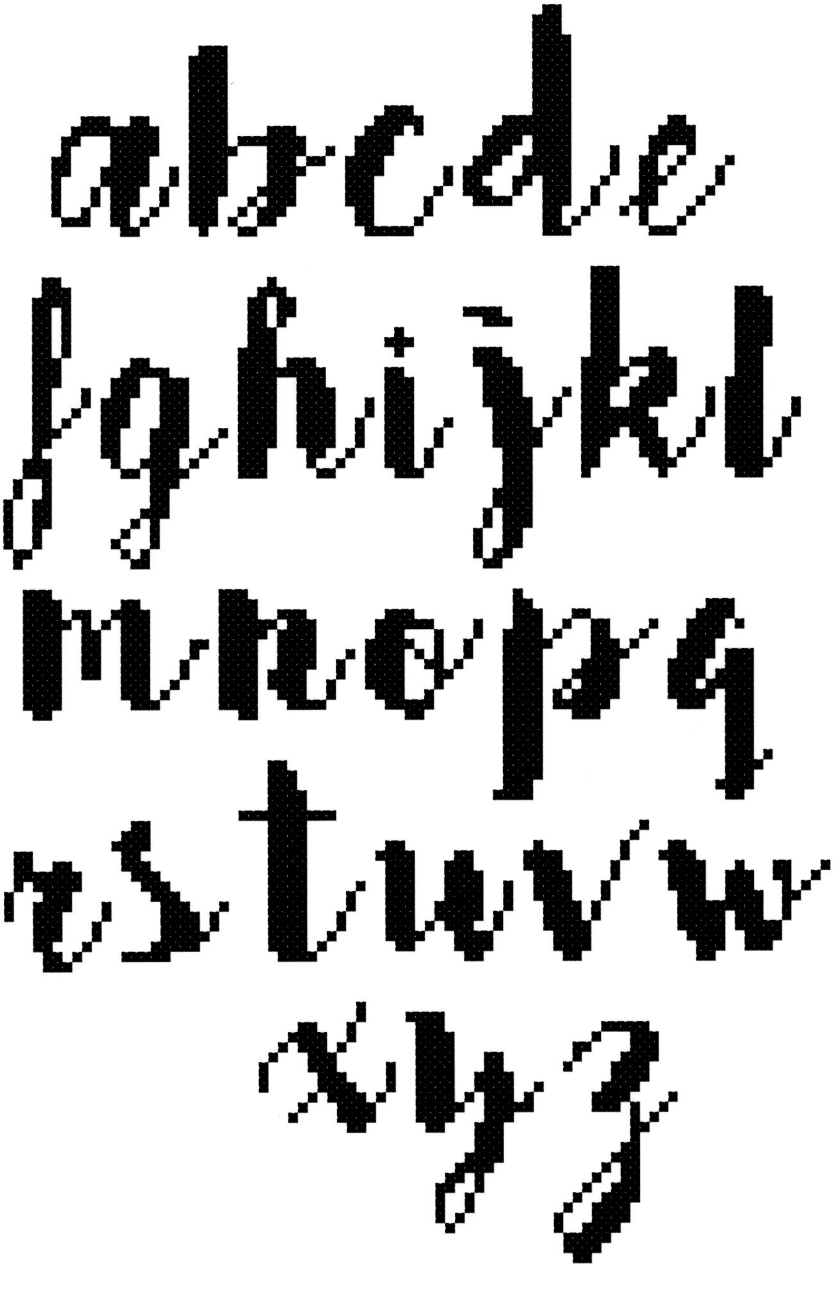

abcdef
ghijkl
mnopqr
stuvw
xyz

ABCDEF
GHIJKL
MNOPQRS
TUVWXYZ
12345
67890

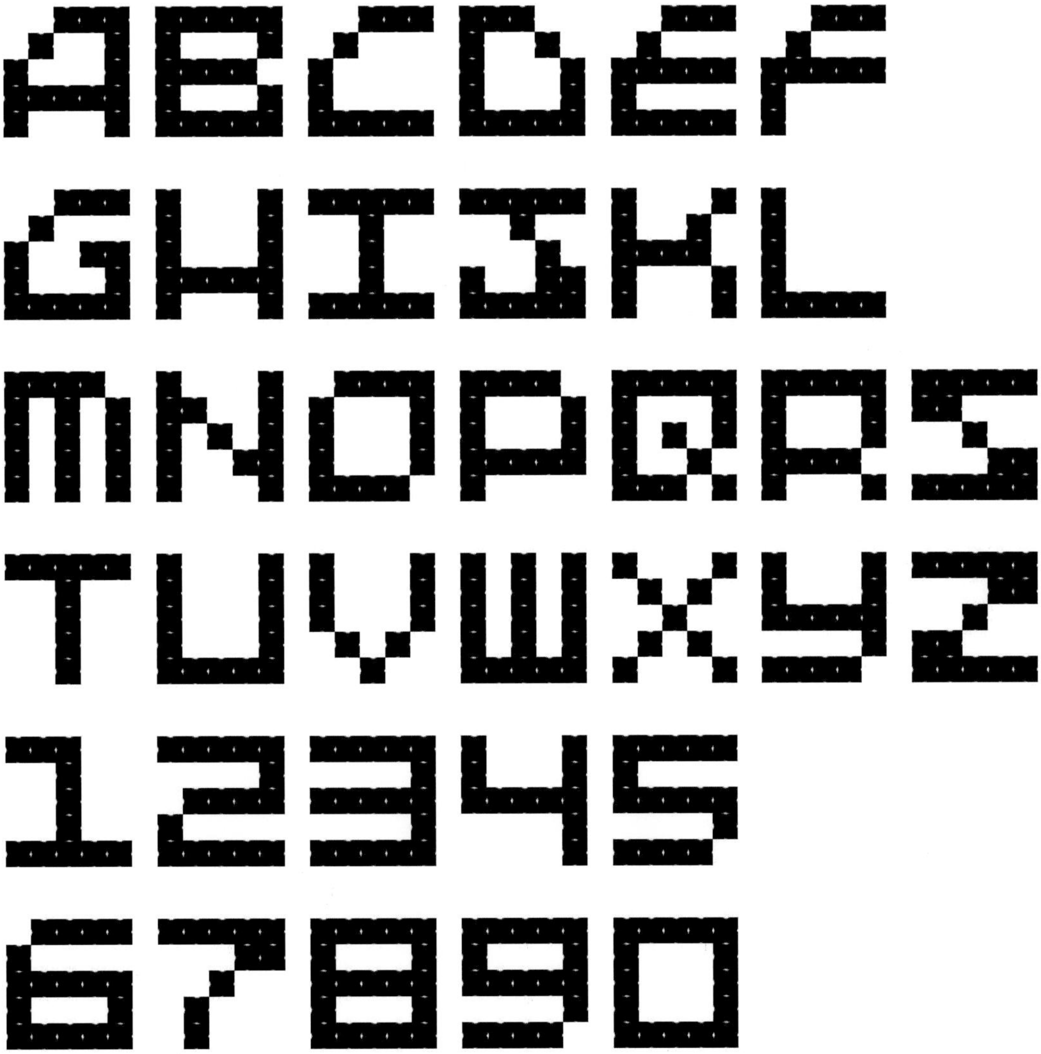

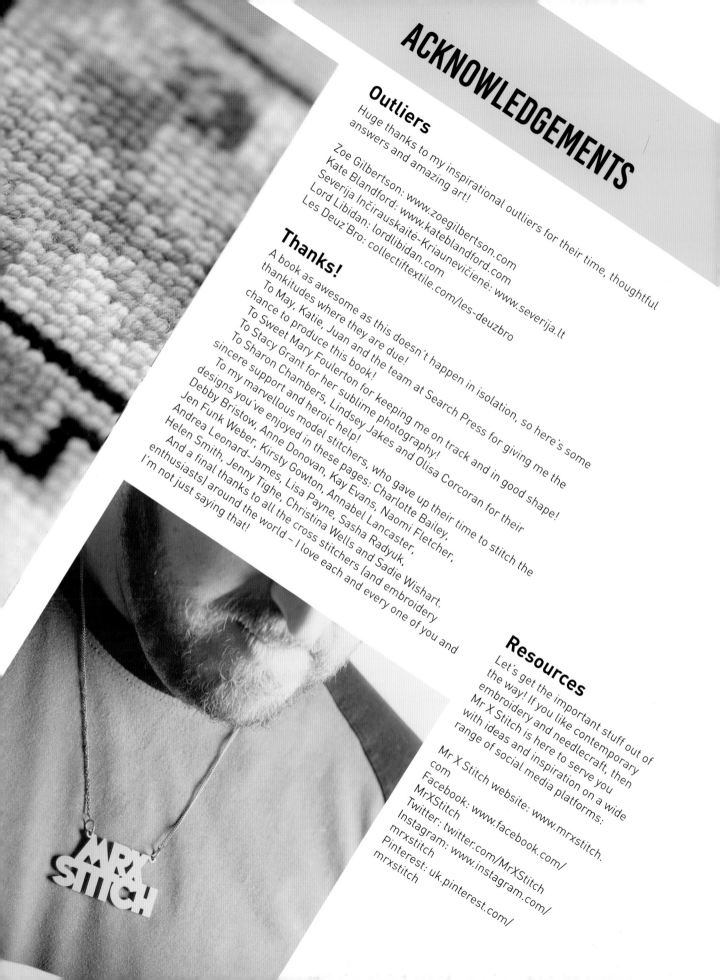

ACKNOWLEDGEMENTS

Outliers

Huge thanks to my inspirational outliers for their time, thoughtful answers and amazing art!

Zoe Gilbertson: www.zoegilbertson.com
Kate Blandford: www.kateblandford.com
Severija Inčirauskaitė-Kriaunevičienė: www.severija.lt
Lord Libidan: lordlibidan.com
Les Deuz'Bro: collectiftextile.com/les-deuzbro

Thanks!

A book as awesome as this doesn't happen in isolation, so here's some thankitudes where they are due!

To May, Katie, Juan and the team at Search Press for giving me the chance to produce this book!
To Sweet Mary Foulerton for keeping me on track and in good shape!
To Stacy Grant for her sublime photography!
To Sharon Chambers, Lindsey Jakes and Olisa Corcoran for their sincere support and heroic help!
To my marvellous model stitchers, who gave up their time to stitch the designs you've enjoyed in these pages: Charlotte Bailey, Debby Bristow, Anne Donovan, Kay Evans, Naomi Fletcher, Jen Funk Weber, Kirsty Gowton, Annabel Lancaster, Andrea Leonard-James, Lisa Payne, Sasha Radyuk, Helen Smith, Jenny Tighe, Christina Wells and Sadie Wishart.
And a final thanks to all the cross stitchers (and embroidery enthusiasts) around the world – I love each and every one of you and I'm not just saying that!

Resources

Let's get the important stuff out of the way! If you like contemporary embroidery and needlecraft, then Mr X Stitch is here to serve you with ideas and inspiration on a wide range of social media platforms:

Mr X Stitch website: www.mrxstitch.com
Facebook: www.facebook.com/MrXStitch
Twitter: twitter.com/MrXStitch
Instagram: www.instagram.com/mrxstitch
Pinterest: uk.pinterest.com/mrxstitch

INDEXXXXXXXXXXXXXXXXXXXXXXX

a
addiction 80
Adobe Illustrator 55
ampersand 42

b
back 32
backstitch 25
Bargello 42, 54, 55
Bayeux Tapestry 46, 131
Betsy Greer 83
blackwork 80
bobbin box 15
bobbin winder 15

c
California poppy 40
coaster 128
colour 36, 100
    graduation 47
    hue 38
    primary 38
    saturation 38
    secondary 38
    spectrum 38
    tertiary 38
    value 38
    wheel 40
Concern Worldwide 83
cosplay 64
craftivism 83
Craftivist Collective 83
cross stitch:
    bottom stitch 20
    top stitch 20
Cthulhu 46

d
dahlia 40
decoupage 29
design software 116
3D 25, 76, 78, 80, 117, 120, 134

e
embroidery hoop 20, 28
embroidery
    as an art form 86
    as therapy 79
Empire State Building 58

f
fabric 14
    Aida 14
    count 99
    evenweave 14
    needlepoint canvas 14
    paper interface 14, 120
    soluble plastic interface 14, 120
    waste canvas 14
fight-or-flight response 79

finishing off 24, 122
framing 28, 33
    lattice method 29–31

g
Game of Thrones 64
geek stitching 68
geometric 42, 50
GitD, see *thread, glow-in-the-dark*
gizmos 15, 102
Grayson Perry 86
Great Tapestry of Scotland 46

h
Harry Potter 64

k
Kate Blandford 72
Kirstie Allsopp 112

l
laying tool 15
Les Deuz'Bro 132
light 17
    clip-on light 17
    daylight 17
    daylight light bullb 17
    head torch 17
Lord Libidan 116, 122
Lord of the Rings 64

m
MacStitch 55
masking tape 30
Michele Carragher 64
mindfulness 76
Mona Lisa 116
My Little Pony 68

n
needles 12
    ivory 46
needle minder 16
New York 58

o
ombre 47
outlier/s 8, 54, 72, 86, 90, 122, 132

p
painting by numbers 20
PCStitch 94
photorealism 112
Picasso 108
pincushion 16
pop art 40, 108, 128
pop culture 8, 64, 68, 116

r
Royal School of Needlework 127

s
Sarah Corbett 83
sci-fi 64
scissors 15
Severija Inčirauskaitė-Kriaunevičienė
                                        90, 120
Stitch for Syria 83
stitches
    quarter stitch 50
    three-quarter stitch 50, 94, 108,
                                        120
stitchgasm 8
stitching on metal 91, 127, 133
stitching on plastic 122

t
techniques:
    loop technique 13, 22
    railroading 15, 112
    separating the strands 13
    waste knot technique 23
technology 94
Teenage Mutant Ninja Turtles 72
The Dark Crystal 64
thread:
    Anchor 13
    DMC 13
    glow-in-the-dark 14, 58, 64,
        68, 70, 72, 73
    Kreinik 13, 58
thread conditioner 16
thread cutter 16
Tracey Emin 86
travelling 63
typography 38

u
upcycling 29

w
washing your work 27
wellbeing 79
wheedle the needle 24, 33, 50
Whitby Abbey 112
wifi password 68
Wikipedia 38, 42, 46, 76

y
Yorkshire Fair 112
YouTube 26

z
Zoe Gilbertson 54

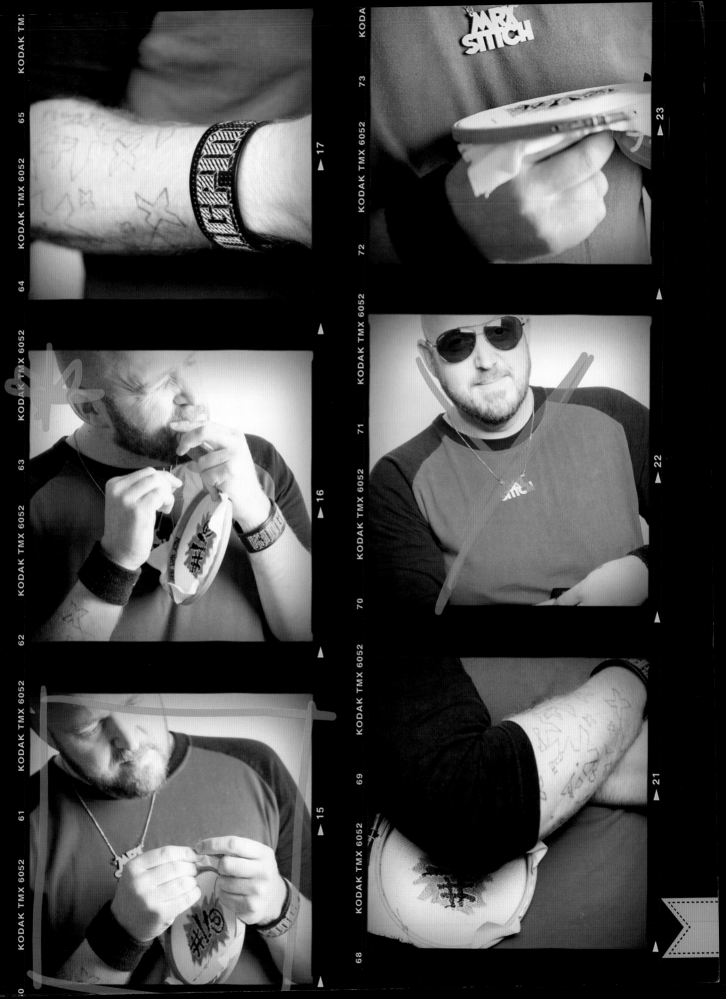